# RESTORING FIRST CENTURY EVANGELISM

FOR AN EFFECTIVE PROGRAM IN SOUL-WINNING
THROUGH
THE REDISCOVERY OF THE WITNESSING POWER OF THE EARLY CHURCH

*EVANGELISM TEXT BOOK AND TRAINING MANUAL*

By
## WILLIAM H. MAYFIELD, D.D., Ph.D.

A Division of Standard Publishing
Cincinnati, Ohio
40-004

Library of Congress Catalog Card Number: 74-81096

ISBN: 0-87239-015-2

© 1974
The STANDARD PUBLISHING Company
Cincinnati, Ohio
*Printed in U.S.A.*

*"Go ye into all the world . . ."*

**Highest point of Jerusalem's
Mount of Olives**

Believed to be the exact site of the
ascension, and the place where Jesus
gave His Great Commission
(Matthew 28:18-20; Acts 1:8, 9).

*EVANGELISM*
*IS*
*LOVE IN ACTION*

WHM

*This book is lovingly dedicated to
two great congregations of Christians who cooperated
fully in carrying out this plan for evangelism:*

*Eau Gallie Christian Church
Melbourne, Florida*

*First Christian Church
Elizabethton, Tennessee*

William H. Mayfield, born in Tulsa, Oklahoma, began his ministerial studies at The Cincinnati Bible Seminary in 1945 after nearly five years in the military service. He flew thirty-two combat missions in Europe as a B-26 crew member. In 1946 he was married to Kay Massey of Harriman, Tennessee. Both he and Mrs. Mayfield earned the A.B. degree from The Cincinnati Bible Seminary and the M.A. from Butler University. After securing also the B.D. degree, Dr. Mayfield received his Ph.D. degree in the field of philosophy from Indiana University in 1953. The D.D. was conferred by Milligan College in 1971. He is in his twenty-sixth year as a full time minister as of this year, 1973. He is a part-time college instructor, now with Milligan College. He has ministered in Indiana, Tennessee and Florida. He is now full time minister of the First Christian Church in Elizabethton, Tennessee. Mrs. Mayfield teaches in the public schools and is a part-time lesson writer for Standard Publishing.

# FOREWORD

In this the church of the latter days, bold ventures in evangelism are imperative for survival. Jesus' Great Commission is voiced with just this kind of urgency.

If I should refuse to be inconvenienced by the accident victim in danger of dying in my street and should neglect to summon aid, I would be guilty of a most dastardly dereliction of duty. But even more terrible would be my dereliction if I should neglect to help the soul who is in need of redemptive aid.

If the Bible is true concerning the two, and only two, after death alternatives (Heaven or Hell for ever and ever), and if acceptance of the Gospel of Jesus Christ makes the difference between these awesome alternatives, is not evangelism the first priority business facing the church? We may be weaker than justified in many areas, but we cannot afford to be weak in the evangelism of souls which Christ commanded in His final commission. This would be the ultimate in dereliction. And sad to say much, if not most, of Christendom is going this ultimate.

The author has for three years as a minister-evangelist used the plan described in this book. It has worked in two ministries and is continuing to work. In three years 529 souls have been added. This is an average of 176 additions per year (one year surpassed 200). In this period (1970-72) 290 were added by baptism (average of 97 per year) and 239 were added by transfer (average of 80 per year). Re-dedications are not counted, but they were many in number. The last three years have shown an increase of 80% in the number of souls won as compared with averages before 1970, the year the plan was put into practice. We confidently look forward to even better statistics as the number of soul-winners in the congregation increases. The glory belongs to God Who gives the increase. We highly recommend the restoration of the personal evangelism of the first century church.

William H. Mayfield
April, 1973

# CONTENTS

*CHAPTER ONE*

## THE IDEAL OF RESTORING FIRST CENTURY EVANGELISM

What can be of greater importance to the Kingdom of God in this, the last third of the twentieth century, than a method of evangelism that will work?

The philosophy of the restoration movement is sound. The appeal to return to the Bible in doctrine and practice is clearly valid. Whether restorationism is a dead ideology or a dynamic movement depends upon evangelism. When we enjoy the blessing of being of one mind concerning the Biblical plan of salvation, we take on a kind of spontaneous identity as a fellowship. But of what real value is such a fellowship if its message is not effectively communicated to a lost world?

I have never met a Christian brother or sister who denied the value of evangelism. Nor have I ever met one who did not agree that we need to evangelize more effectively. The answer to this universal desire to see the church successfully engaged in evangelism lies within the framework of "restoration" - - i.e., restoring the evangelistic methods of the first century church. Let us look at what happened in the early days of the church:

1.    The resurrected Lord commissioned His disciples to witness: "Go ye into all the world and preach the gospel" (Mark 16:15), and "ye shall be witnesses unto me" (Acts 1:8).

2.    The first witnessing at Pentecost resulted in 3000 conversions (Acts 2:41).

3.    The then formed church of Christ was a fellowship given to witnessing, which is evidenced by the fact that 5000 more were added shortly after Pentecost (Acts 4:4).

4.    The fires of personal evangelism continued to spread, for "believers were the more added to the Lord, multitudes both men and women" (Acts 5:14). The number is not cited. After the 3000 and 5000 - - "multitudes!"

5.    One chapter later in Acts and still probably no later than 33 A.D. according to Bible chronologists, "The word of God increased; and the number of the disciples multiplied in Jerusalem greatly; and a great company of the priests were obedient to the faith " (Acts 6:7).

6.    As we move forward in time to about 64 A.D., some thirty years later, Paul was able to write that the gospel "was preached to every creature which is under heaven" (Colossians 1:23), as Jesus had commanded (Mark 16:15).

7.    By the end of the second century A.D. the Christian elder Tertullian (160-220 A.D.), it is reported, wrote a message to an official of Emperor Severus of Rome to the effect that - -

we Christians are everywhere in the Empire - - we are in your cities - - we are in your villages - - we are scattered throughout your countryside - - we are in your armies - - we are even in your senate.

8.    The world was turned upside down for Jesus (Acts 17:6) in a little more than a generation.  How did this incredible thing happen?  There is one answer.  The message of the Christ is true and the Christians of the first century were totally dedicated to witnessing.  What was their secret?  It is reflected in Acts 8:4.  As the effects of persecution were being felt by the church, "they that were scattered abroad went everywhere preaching the word."

9.    Hence we conclude, evangelism was the first business of the early church.  If the world is won, evangelism must become the first business of today's church.  This will radically revolutionize most established local church programs.  May God send such a revolution!


## PURPOSE

The purpose of this book is to aid in this needed restoration of the power of first century evangelism.

In my personal ministry of some twenty-six years I have continually sought better methods of evangelism.  Down through the years our ministry has been highlighted by the presence of some of our nation's best known evangelists.  These dedicated men led us in successful revival campaigns preceded by weeks of intensive preparation.  We rejoiced at the resulting harvest.  But after the revival we saw our people go on "sit-down strike," apparently weary in well-doing.  Our evangelists were tops, and we still use them.  But the problem that I faced was keeping this kind of effective evangelism going around the calendar.  This is the great need of the church.

There are certain musts if evangelism is to be year-round and permanent in the church.  The preacher must stay fired-up for evangelism and his people must share this zeal from January 1 to December 31 every year.  The only way this can happen is for the church members to become as involved in evangelism as the preacher and as capable of bringing souls to decisions for Christ. If we truly accept the principle of the universal priesthood of all believers (I Peter 2:9), and reject the man-conceived clergy-laity dichotomy, this will have to be our goal.


## ARRIVING AT A WORKABLE PROGRAM

Early in 1970 Brother Olin Hay of Tampa, Florida, shared

some moments with me. He had just returned from the now famous evangelism clinic in Fort Lauderdale, Florida. He was very enthusiastic about the "Evangelism Explosion" program of Dr. James Kennedy. I knew immediately that if there were something there that would improve my evangelism, it would take first place on my agenda. Soon thereafter I secured Dr. Kennedy's book, *EVANGELISM EXPLOSION*. It was money well spent. I highly recommend it to anyone interested in improving the evangelistic effectiveness of his church. The methodology advanced in this work definitely approaches that of the first century church. I owe a great debt of gratitude to Dr. Kennedy for the benefit I have received from his work. It has triggered many of the ideas that we will be writing about.

As I read Dr. Kennedy's book, I became deeply conscious of something that I thought I had believed all along - - i.e., New Testament church evangelism included all Christians - - not just a fraternity of preachers. This was the "missing key" - - every Christian should be trained to evangelize as effectively as the preacher.

In April of that year Preacher J. Pat Carrington and I visited the Coral Ridge congregation in Fort Lauderdale and gained permission from the gracious Dr. Kennedy to call with one of his trainers. This was on a scheduled calling night. We saw the program in action. We saw scores of "laymen" on fire to evangelize. By February of 1971 I was a participant in Dr. Kennedy's annual evangelism clinic. Even though I had already started the plan in my ministry several months earlier, the clinic enabled me to improve greatly the evangelistic program of my church.

More fully than ever before, I came to the conviction that one of the preacher's first duties is to convince his people that personal evangelism is every Christian's business. This is the key to winning the world to Jesus Christ. Mr., Mrs., and Miss Average Church Member must: (1) be convinced that it is his or her personal duty to witness to others; (2) be willing and desirous to learn how to do it effectively and (3) be willing to get involved in a definite program of personal evangelism.

We have known intellectually that Christ has commissioned His church to evangelize the world but we have done so little about it. This important job cannot be left to the preachers alone. If the world is to be won to Jesus, so-called "laymen" as well as preachers must know how to evangelize effectively and must actually do so.

When we attended the first session of the 1971 Coral Ridge clinic on evangelism in Fort Lauderdale, Florida, led by Dr. Kennedy, we noticed a large computer in the banquet hall of the hotel where we were assembled. Digital numbers were advancing at a rapid rate. This dramatized that even as we sat there the world population was soaring. Dr. Kennedy reminded us that if the church continues with the theory of evangelism which it has held in the past - - the traditional "let the preacher do it" philosophy - - in a generation Christianity will be only an obscure minority movement. The population increase will have left us far behind. However, if one dedicated Christian will in a six month period of time win another person to Christ, AND TEACH THIS NEW CONVERT TO BE A SOUL-WINNER, and if the two will do the same thing during the next six month period, the four the following six months, etc. - - in sixteen short years the world will be won. The explosion of evangelism can catch up with the population explosion in just one generation!

To do this, the traditional view of the minister must be radically revolutionized. The idea that "our minister is here to serve us" must be replaced with the concept that "our minister is here to train us to do the job that we Christians have been commanded by our Lord to do."

As an instructor in evangelism, the minister teaches more by actual demonstration than by lecturing in a classroom situation. Take the hypothetical case of the student pilot. Can you imagine his taking forty hours of flight theory in ground school after which he is told to enter the aircraft for the first time and solo? Tragically, this theory of teaching has been too often attempted in training soul winners. In view of this, it is not hard to understand why the average church program in personal evangelism ends in utter frustration.

Christians learn to witness by actually doing it. A well trained soul-winner takes with him (or her) two trainees. The team goes into the field to witness for Christ. After weekly training for approximately four months, trainees have learned to win souls. They have learned by actually doing it. Just as the student pilot learns to fly, not on the ground, but at dual controls 3000 feet in the air, the trainee in evangelism learns to witness by observation and actual participation. After receiving this on-the-field training, learners in turn may themselves become teachers.

## AVOIDING MISTAKES

A look at our personal evangelism programs in the past can make us ashamed of tragic failures. A preacher can prepare and effectively deliver soul-arousing messages on personal evangelism. Such messages are a first step, but only a first step, toward an effective program in witnessing. It is easier by far to preach the principles of soul-winning than it is to put them effectively into practice in a year-round church program.

## 1. A Typical Mistake

No doubt a thousand preachers have had experiences similar to the following:

Being sold on the idea that every Christian should witness for Christ, the preacher delivers a strong Scriptural sermon on the subject. He announces a series of classes on personal evangelism to meet each Sunday evening at 6:00. He also announces calling for Tuesday nights from 7:00 to 9:00. At the Sunday session, he tells them all about how to win souls. On Tuesday he sends them out for calling. The class starts with forty and within six weeks dwindles to four. Tuesday night visitation follows the same numerical pattern.

The frustrated preacher says, "To heck with it! Maybe I can find a job teaching evangelism in a Bible College!" (For the sake of our ministerial students, we hope not!)

What was wrong? Is the failure due to the preacher's lack of dedication? Not at all! Is it due to a theological deficiency on his part? This also is not the answer. It actually boils down to a lack of understanding of people and their weaknesses and to a fallacy in method.

Even the novice minister soon discovers that a mere asking for volunteers in a program of the church is asking for failure. Also he soon learns that even when workers are secured they will not long remain secured unless the job is (1) spelled out in detail and (2) carefully directed. Please allow these principles to soak in. They can make the difference between success and failure.

## 2. Mistakes in Recruitment and Training

One common mistake involves the failure to recruit properly. Another mistake involves a fallacy in training methods. A trainee for soul-winning must be definitely recruited even if he comes as a volunteer. Each trainee should sign a recruitment card for a definite tour of duty (say, for four months). The amount of time involved each week during the period should be clearly defined. In our local program we employ two and one-half hours weekly - - one-half hour in class immediately followed by two hours of witnessing. Avoid being indefinite in the "nailing-down" of personnel.

## 3. Academic Mistakes

Also avoid the mistake that arises from the notion that personal evangelism can be learned in a classroom. It cannot! The trainee learns by going into the homes of prospects with a trainer. Insurance salesmen have known this for years. It is time, past time, for the church to abandon unrealistic methods that won't work and to involve itself in a training program for soul-winners geared to human nature.

If we are truly convicted about personal evangelism, we must avoid allowing Satan-inspired discouragements to slow-up or kill the program after it has been started. This is an ever present threat. All of this means that evangelism must become and must remain the FIRST BUSINESS OF THE CHURCH.

## MATTER OF PRIORITY

The preacher must be sold on the philosophy that it is his high priority duty to train his people in personal witnessing to the point that these properly equipped soul-winners are capable of bringing a person clear through to a positive obedient decision for Christ, if the person is at all receptive to the Gospel.

## SOME IMPORTANT CONSIDERATIONS

1. This training program must take a first place priority in the affairs of the church.

2. It must be kept before the people, who are being sought out continually for recruitment.

3. It is important to avoid the ever-present danger in the church of allowing less important programs to infringe on evangelism or even push it to the side-lines. This sort of thing has in many congregations caused the eventual death of active evangelism.

4. Above all, keep the program in personal evangelism and evangelism training going on a year-round basis. Don't allow discouragements to slow it up or stop it. The secret of eventual success is staying with it. There will be times of high spirit and long periods of low. However, perseverance pays off.

5. Again let us emphasize that evangelism is every Christian's business. A one-man preacher team will involve less than one per cent of the church. Militarily speaking, this method spells certain defeat. It is vitally important to properly train soul-winners.

6. Always keep God at the center. Prayer and faith are definite requisites for success.

*CHAPTER TWO*

## PREPARING FOR EFFECTIVE PERSONAL EVANGELISM

Preparation for effective personal evangelism in the local church program must be accomplished in at least two areas. First, the preacher needs to be both sold on and equipped for soul-winning himself and must be able to teach it to others. Second, the congregation must be prepared for this kind of evangelistic venture. Involvement in such an adventure can pump new vigor into the spiritually tired blood of a preacher dying of boredom in a humdrum ministry. It can put new life-blood into a church that has stagnated into the mere status of a community institution. Permanent, not seasonal, revival can be the wonderful result.

## THE MINISTER PREPARED FOR EVANGELISM

The faith and vision of a congregation is not likely to be any greater than that of its leadership. Too many enter the ministry with ambitions no higher than that of becoming a senior minister staff-man administering the affairs of an established church. After all, the honor and the status of the calling is a great nourisher of the ego. The minister needs first to look at himself and his calling. Only by looking to Jesus can it all come into proper perspective.

Even though the clergy-laity dichotomy is more traditional than Biblical, the church from its beginning until now has had a definite need for dedicated leadership (Ephesians 4:11-13; I Timothy 3). Elders, deacons and teachers of local congregations may or may not be fired-up for evangelism. Many who are not would like to be. A realistic look at the contemporary scene in Christendom, with its lack of effective soul-winning energy should clue in any preacher to his greatest challenge - - i.e., restoring the evangelism of the first century church.

That the called man of God should be completely converted, Scripturally and experientially born again in Jesus, is an indisputable truism. His prayer life and devotional life must be real and consistent. He must be sold completely on the saving power of the Gospel.

Now, how may he best view the priorities of his calling? As a true Bible believing minister he wants to excel in soul-winning on the field and in the pulpit. If this is a fine goal, how much finer to project toward teaching a congregation of Bible believing people to join with him in the thrilling adventure of soul-winning?

It can happen if, and only if, he begins with a real personal closeness to the Lord. The plan for lasting evangelism must begin in prayer and continue in more prayer. By seeking the power and the leading of the Holy Spirit, and by looking with confidence to God for this power, the minister's involvement in His commissioned work can lead to victory. His goal is to restore the evangelism as well as the doctrine of the early church.

Obviously then, the called leader must know how to present the Gospel effectively. However, many have conceived the challenge as mainly exhortation from the pulpit. No doubt about it, strong pulpit ability to preach the Gospel is highly desirable and is greatly needed in Christendom. Tragically, though, many a conservative minister can tell it from the pulpit, but hasn't the foggiest notion how to present the good news convincingly to a person face to face. His evangelistic calls are little more than small talk which ends with an invitation to come visit church. His unworkable theory seems to be in effect: Invite the sinner to church, hope he stumbles into the sanctuary in answer to the invitation and hope he can be won by pulpit preaching. Why should a sinner want to visit a church? Only a pitifully small per cent choose to attend. Even fewer will walk down the aisle during the invitation hymn.

The minister will lead his people to evangelistic action if, and only if, he himself learns to witness effectively on a person to person level. He must come to grips with the challenge, and he must learn to win souls by doing it day in and day out. It must be a blue Monday to bright Sunday experience. It is important for him to have the Biblical plan of salvation in mind to the point that it is part of him. He should be able to present it to an individual with the same confidence (though with a somewhat different method of delivery) as in the pulpit. It should be followed by the definite seeking of a decision for Christ.

The minister desiring to convert his congregation to active personal evangelism must then be an effective personal evangelist. If he is not, learning it and practicing it is the first challenge facing him. Chapter Four deals with the actual presentation of the Gospel to individuals in simple but effective language. The minister must learn to do this before he can set up a successful church program in witnessing.

The preacher's preparation should include the study of helpful material, especially the Word of God, as well as the practice of actual witnessing and seeking decisions for Christ. Study of materials on evangelism, such as this one, should be helpful. However, he should avoid trying to amalgamate several different plans. This rarely works because of the too complicated plan that emerges.

Effective witnessing experience, fervent prayer and careful planning can put the minister on the right road toward leading his flock in the thrilling experience of personal evangelism. If winning a soul is the greatest thrill of the ministry, should not this thrill be shared with all willing Christians?

## THE CONGREGATION PREPARED FOR EVANGELISM

After the minister becomes sold on the ideal that evangelism is indeed the first business of the church, he is ready to groom his congregation for the thrilling venture. This cannot be accomplished by casual planning and occasional announcements. It must begin with a definite decision to make personal evangelism the top priority "must" in the local church program. The minister is sold on the proposition and endeavors to pass it on to his church leadership.

## SELL THE LEADERSHIP

Wise strategy backed by prayer will begin to take shape. A well chosen evangelism committee should be prominent in the church committee structure. Heart to heart, fortified with prayer and an open Bible, the preacher sells his committee. The evangelism committee sells the elders first, and then both elders and deacons. The congregation, then, sees this as much more than a preacher's project.

## A DEFINITE PLAN OF ACTION

A definite calendar needs to be adopted which includes various target dates - - (1) the date to present the plan to the congregation and to begin placing the projected soul-winning program at the top of the church prayer list, and (2) the date to begin recruitment (although the first round begins with just a few hand picked trainees). In anticipation of the target date for the actual program, a series of Gospel sermons on evangelism should be sounded forth from the pulpit. Prayer enlistment from both participants and non-participants in the training program is essential. The entire congregation can be enlisted for prayer. If the church is praying for evangelism, its membership will be more recruitable for evangelism as the program progresses.

Some six weeks of intensive preparation should proceed the starting date. A good motivator to use is the fifty minute sound movie, "Like A Mighty Army." This film is the story of Dr. James Kennedy's "Evangelism Explosion" program in Fort Lauderdale, Florida. It can be secured through Gospel film supply houses on a rental basis. It can be shown a few weeks before the program begins in the local church. It emphasizes the importance of effective "lay-evangelism" and dramatizes the thrill of witnessing. It shows the validity of the principle that Christians can win souls to Christ if properly trained to do so. This can give aid to the minister in selling the congregation on the proposition that personal evangelism is every Christian's business.

## CAREFUL AND INTENSIVE RECRUITMENT

Starting with too many trainees on the first round can weaken the program by producing poorly trained personnel. Since one trainer can train only two persons at a time, the first training round will not involve a large number. The recruits may therefore be hand picked. However, as the second and third rounds approach, the number should be steadily increasing.

Printed enlistment cards should be plentiful. These may be displayed from the pulpit and made ready in the foyer. Seek to enlist the needed number of trainees (two per trainer) from volunteers. However, it will probably be necessary to encounter several people face to face to lay the opportunity upon their hearts.

Every effort should be made to enlist the church leaders. It is desirable to get elders, deacons and teachers in on the action early. If these leaders cannot be recruited, seek other trainees and pray that the leaders will soon catch the vision of personal evangelism.

Personal appeals before elders' and deacons' groups, before committees and ladies' organizations can bring in some results. In addition, encounter people personally whom you consider good prospects for soul-winning. Put your trainers to work also in seeking new trainees. After two years and four full rounds in the program you may need to find fifty or more new workers for the next round of training. Energetic and prayerful efforts in seeking these workers will keep the program alive.

Adequate preparation is vital to the success of your soul-winning program. Evangelism is the heart beat of a living, functioning church. It is everybody's business, from the minister to the eldership and deaconship and on to the entire constituency of the church. The Good News of the Gospel is the most glorious message humanity has ever been offered. But of what good is it, if it is not communicated to a lost world? "How shall they believe in Him of whom they have not heard?" (Romans 10:14).

*ELIZABETHTON, TENNESSEE — 1972.   Graduates of the second round of Evangelism Training holding their certificates. Chairman of Evangelism, Luther Hayes, is pictured in the center, with Bobby Woods, Chairman of Youth Evangelism, on the far right.   Preacher William Mayfield is pictured at the center rear.*

*CHAPTER THREE*

## IMPLEMENTING THE PERSONAL EVANGELISM PROGRAM

A cause can be lost in the abyss that lies between the mountain tops of theory and action. Most grand ideas do not reach the lofty peak of realization. I can think of no greater tragedy than for this fate to befall Christ's plan for evangelizing the world.

Kierkegaard used to relate his parable of the barnyard geese. Farmer Olsen kept them well fed and well fenced-in. Among their number was a preacher goose. Each time a flock of wild geese flew over he was inspired to preach. He would struggle up on a stump and call his companions to church. "We should be ashamed," he would say. "Our forefathers flew through the heavens with grace and freedom, and here we are too over-fed to fly over this fence. We should be up and flying." About this time Farmer Olsen would appear with his sack of grain. Can you guess who was the first to the feeding trough? That's right, the preacher goose was the first one to stuff himself. All were doomed to the ground and eventually to the chopping block because of their empty theory.

If there is one area above all others in which the preacher needs preaching to, it concerns his failure to actuate theoretically good plans. During the past three years I have talked with scores of ministers who intend to begin a training program in evangelism for their people. Few of this number have done little more than talk about it. Others have started programs but with too many fears and reservations, or with insufficient plans and preparation. Still others have started programs but have failed to keep them alive.

We would like to share a workable plan for training personal evangelists in the church and for enabling them actually to win souls to the Lord. Church members can be taught to share the Gospel with others and to bring souls to positive decisions for Christ.

Every minister early discovers that it is necessary to work close to the calendar. Good plans are in the hopper but in this state they represent only potential. The move from potentiality to actuality is accomplished by "zeroing-in" on well thought out "target-dates."

In this program of "Restoring First Century Evangelism" three stages are necessary: (1) The Planning Period - - forming the plans prayerfully and deciding on target-dates; (2) The Preparation Period - - making preparations for the implementation of the planned program; and (3) The Program Period - - the starting of the program itself on the target-date. These three steps mark the difference between half-hearted, half-prepared, "half-cocked" programs geared to failure and programs which are carried to successful realization. If any program in the church needs to succeed, it is most certainly that of evangelism. In the evangelism program here described, the planning period comes once before the first round of preparation and training. After that, the cycle is in two parts: (1) The Preparation Period and (2) The Program itself.

Church years, like corporation years, can start on almost any calendar month. However, we have found it most convenient simply to use the January-December calendar year for the personal evangelism of our congregation. The program then can easily be re-cycled each year. The year is divided into four unequal parts - - two months, four months, two months and four months. Each of the two month periods are devoted to preparation, while the four month periods are devoted to the personal evangelism training. Hence, January and February are recruitment months. March through June are dedicated to the training-witnessing program. July and August are for preparation, and the actual program is again conducted September through December. The re-cycling actually occurs twice a year. We are dealing with two six month blocks of time each year. These blocks are divided into a two month period followed by a four month period.

The two month preparation period should include strong Bible sermons on personal evangelism. These messages ought to challenge Christians to want to witness. Also during at least the first preparation period, it would be beneficial to show the film referred to earlier, "Like A Mighty Army." During the last half of the preparation period recruitment of participants in the training-witnessing program should be completed. Let us look at what can be a typical six months' calendar:

# TYPICAL CALENDAR

# TWO MONTHS OF PREPARATION

**ANY YEAR**
**January and February**
**July and August**

## July

| SUNDAY | MONDAY | TUESDAY | WEDNESDAY | THURSDAY | FRIDAY | SATURDAY |
|---|---|---|---|---|---|---|
| 1 — Diplomas presented to graduates of previous round. Publicize in church and local papers. | 2 | 3 | 4 | 5 | 6 | 7 |
| 8 — Surveying twice each month throughout year - Probably on alternate Sunday afternoons | 9 | 10 | 11 | 12 | 13 | 14 |
| 15 | 16 | 17 | 18 — Recruitment and witnessing program on prayer list each Prayer Meeting night, and Sundays, | 19 | 20 | 21 |
| 22 — Film "Like A Mighty Army" may be shown about this time every year or two. | 23 | 24 | 25 | 26 | 27 | 28 |
| 29 — Sermon on Witnessing | 30 | 31 KEEP RECRUITMENT APPEAL IN CHURCH PAPER AS WELL AS IN ANNOUNCEMENTS | | | | |

# August

| SUNDAY | MONDAY | TUESDAY | WEDNESDAY | THURSDAY | FRIDAY | SATURDAY |
|---|---|---|---|---|---|---|
| | | | 1 | 2 | 3 | 4 |
| | WORKERS ARE SEEKING RECRUITS FOR THE PROGRAM ALL THROUGH THIS MONTH. | | | | | |
| 5 **Sermon on Witnessing. Insert recruitment feelers in bulletins.** | 6 | 7 | 8 | 9 | 10 | 11 |
| | | SECURE NURSERY WORKERS FOR CALLING NIGHTS. ALSO SECURE WORKERS TO PREPARE REFRESHMENTS FOR CHECK-IN TIME AFTER CALLING. | | | | |
| 12 **Sermon on Witnessing. Insert recruitment cards in bulletins.** | 13 | 14 | 15 | 16 | 17 | 18 |
| 19 **Sermon on Witnessing. Insert recruitment cards in bulletins.** | 20 | 21 | 22 | 23 | 24 | 25 |
| | | FINALIZE LIST OF NAMES OF TRAINERS AND RECRUITED TRAINEES, AND PUBLISH. | | | | |
| 26 | 27 | 28 | 29 | 30 | 31 | |
| | | PREPARE WALL CHARTS WITH NAMES OF TRAINERS AND TRAINEES. | | | | |

# FOUR MONTHS TRAINING-WITNESSING PROGRAM

### March through June — and again — September through December
(Let the calendar block in this space represent any of the four training months of each cycle.)

For March, April, May, June — and for — September, October, November, December

| SUNDAY | MONDAY | TUESDAY | WEDNESDAY | THURSDAY | FRIDAY | SATURDAY |
|---|---|---|---|---|---|---|
| | | Training-witnessing program each Tuesday P.M. 7:00-7:30 In class 7:30-9:30 Calling in homes 9:30 Check in at church | | | | 1 |
| 2 Workers' consecration service at beginning of program - on Sunday preceding first calling night. | 3 | 4 | 5 A.M. program for another group 9:30-Noon | 6 Afternoon program for youth 3:30-6:00 | 7 | 8 |
| 9 | 10 | 11 | 12 | 13 | 14 | 15 |
| 16 | 17 | 18 | 19 | 20 | 21 | 22 |
| 23 / 30 | 24 | 25 Last month - final exam - Gospel outline and Scripture written from memory | 26 | 27 | 28 | 29 |

(Some shifting of days may be necessary during Christmas season.)

Class time for first two months involves learning Gospel outline and Scriptures, answering excuses, dealing with special problems, etc. During the last two months each trainee presents Gospel outline to class.

Calling time during first two months — trainees observe as trainer witnesses, however trainees should contribute helpful but limited comments. During the last two months trainees begin making the Gospel presentation in the homes in the presence of trainer.

One half-hour in class.
Two hours calling.

All workers, trainers
and trainees, must be
in class five minutes
early. Every minute
of the half hour must
be used.

Assignment cards for
teams are prepared
ahead of time, for
minimum loss of
time at 7:30 assignment
session.

**FOR AN EVERY YEAR PROGRAM:**
January and February — Preparation Period
March through June — The Program in Evangelism
July and August — Preparation Period
September through December — The Program in Evangelism

# MORE ABOUT RECRUITMENT

A church begins its first venture into "Restoring First Century Evangelism" with just a few hand-picked trainees. The minister, and perhaps his associate, are the first trainers. At most about six, probably less, will graduate from the first four months' training program. Another two months of recruitment will follow in preparation for the next four months. Now from four to six persons plus the preacher(s) can take on two trainees each. This may call for the recruitment of from eight to fourteen on the second round. After two years the church should be seeking up to fifty. Recruitment becomes an increasing challenge.

During each two months of preparation the matter of recruitment should be placed on the church prayer list. This should be done six weeks ahead of the program target date. At least four weeks should be dedicated to the actual securing of the prospective trainees. A "recruitment feeler" insert should be put in the Sunday bulletin a month ahead of the starting date. The "feeler" is not a commitment card but is designed to lay the burden upon the hearts of the people. See Chapter Five on "Helpful Materials" for a sample "feeler" bulletin insert.

These inserts should be taken up by the ushers. The preacher may receive many leads from these "feelers" as to who may be recruited.

Three weeks ahead of the target date, the recruitment card should be inserted in the bulletin. Place a table and chair in the church foyer and appoint someone to receive filled out commitment cards. The card should state the definite dates of the four month tour of duty and should be signed by the recruit. See Chapter Five for a sample card idea.

If after a two Sunday effort, in which both the "feelers" and recruitment cards are used, there is still a shortage of volunteers, the personal contact approach should be intensified. Attempts to enlist elders, deacons and teachers should come before, during and after the congregation-wide enlistment endeavor. Use all of the church leaders obtainable. If these church leaders "drag their feet," don't be discouraged. Recruit anyone who is willing to be involved in this, the greatest work of the church - - personal evangelism. Many of the long-time "pillars" of the church may eventually be won to the program. A glorious blessing awaits the Christian who is willing to learn to witness. Here the thrill of being a Christian truly comes into focus.

Shortly after a group of trainees are graduated they should be given several enlistment cards. Have them again fill out one for the next round of training, during which they can be trainers, and then send them out to seek recruits. If each trainer personally recruits two, this would entirely fill the need for the next round.

# SECURING PROSPECTS

The securing of sufficient prospects is one of the real challenges of the soul-winning program, especially as workers increase in number.

What is a prospect? The word is almost self-defining, but the identifying of prospects is more difficult. How can we determine who is and who is not a potential convert to Christ and a prospective member of the local church? The fact is, we cannot. We deal with an array of people who are not in the Body of Christ. Only by witnessing to these lost or misplaced souls can we even begin to make a tentative determination as to who is and who is not a prospect. Jesus sent His disciples forth to witness to the lost sheep of Israel. He briefed them on what they would encounter. Some would be receptive; some would not. Concerning the latter He said, "Shake off the dust of your feet" (Matthew 10:14). God forbid, however, that we should ever do this prematurely!

A fundamental principle in this program must be - - EVERY LOST PERSON IS A PROSPECT. The idea that only people who have visited the church services are prospects is completely anti-scriptural and is in diametric contradiction to the Great Commission of our Lord. Co-relating to the above principle - - EVERY ONCE BAPTIZED, BUT NOW UNCHURCHED OR INACTIVE, PERSON IS A PROSPECT.

The prospect list on hand in any church is our starter. If one does not exist at all, a list must be started. To this list we add the names and addresses of church visitors. These current visitors are the top priority people on whom we should call.

The silent roll call card in every bulletin is a "must." If members are not involved in filling out these cards, visitors will be less inclined to do so. Everyone should fill out and turn in a silent roll call card. Thus, the visitors are identified and the members are kept in focus as to attendance habits.

Visitors' cards should also be turned in from each Sunday School class. Teachers need to be taught to do this faithfully. The evangelism chairman and minister must receive all of this visitor information early on Monday mornings.

"Prayer and Concern" cards should be in the pew holders. Members should be urged to supply names and addresses of all possible prospects among their family, neighbors and friends. See Chapter Five for card samples.

A large number of prospects can be discovered through the full cooperation of the membership in supplying this vital information. The evangelism committee should also carefully go through the church membership and Sunday School rolls to discover the unsaved and unchurched among the church families.

Every effort needs to be made to secure the names and addresses of all newcomers. If at all possible secure the aid of utility companies. The help of the welcome to new residents organizations can be valuable, even though this channel is usually not as fast as that of the utilities. In some cities there are agencies that will supply newcomers' names to churches. Sometimes there is a fee, but the expenditure for such information is very good stewardship of church funds.

Be ever alert for "hidden" prospects. When a prospect lives at a certain address, there is a great chance that two or three other prospects live at the same address. Also hidden prospects are often found among the neighbors, relatives and friends of known prospects. Discreetly phrased questions concerning this possibility should be asked of the people on whom we call.

If these suggestions are faithfully followed, it will help to keep the prospect file alive and current. If we are truly interested in souls, we should avoid thinking of any prospect, however remote, as a "suspect." Every soul is precious. Every person without Christ is a mission field.


## THE AREA SURVEY

The importance of the religious survey of a city or community cannot be over-emphasized. This is vital for keeping personal evangelism alive.

If there is a cooperative city-wide church survey program going on in your field, you should be in on it. However, these programs are not regularly conducted in most places. In the last analysis, you will probably have to operate the survey from your local church. This should be done annually rather than on a one-time basis.

Survey cards should be printed in large numbers. All necessary information should be on the card, but it should be fairly brief. See Chapter Five for a sample survey card.

If your area is larger than 15,000 in population, the survey program will be going on most of the year and hence will be a continuing one. Survey sessions can be held on alternate Sunday afternoons, or twice per month. The two hours from 2:30 to 4:30 are ideal. If one or two Sunday School classes are enlisted for each session, any given individual will not be called upon to survey more than about six times a year. As the survey sessions are announced and promoted, this should be pointed out. If necessary, have the individuals in these participating classes sign up for definite dates to work.

The surveyors need to be instructed each session as to how to proceed. Each worker should be given several cards and sent out to go from door to door on a certain assigned street. Another worker can cover the opposite side of the street. It is not the purpose of the survey to visit or to witness. It is simply for the gaining of information. Instruct the worker to knock on the door and seek to obtain the desired information as he stands at the door. Entering the home would take too much time. The visitation comes later. Names of parents and names and ages of children should be obtained. This information is sought after a brief but friendly introduction that may go something like this:

"Hello! I'm Bill Smith from the First Christian Church. We are taking a religious survey in our community. May I have just a minute or two of your time?"

After this he asks for names and proceeds to fill out the rest of the card. There should be a place on the card to indicate whether church membership is of an active nature or not. A person who is a member somewhere, but not active, may be considered as much of a prospect as the non-church members. Thus information concerning active church membership, if any, is of vital importance.

The brief interview should be ended with a pleasant expression of thanks. If the person interviewed is a prospect and seems fairly receptive, an invitation to visit church can be given. On the card the prospect should be evaluated by the worker as being "excellent", "good" or "fair." This, of course, should be done after the worker leaves the porch and not in the person's presence.

"Not at home" should be written at the top of the card and the address filled in at each house where this applies. These cards should be stacked separately for a second attempt later.

Before the survey begins, it is wise for the minister to draft a letter to the mayor and the chief of police informing them of the survey program. This is for protection in case church surveying is erroneously confused with soliciting. File carbons of these letters.

All prospective names from the surveying should be entered on cards for the calling file and then processed for the witnessing program. When the Gospel is later presented, some of these people can be won to Christ even if they have never before visited the local church.


## THE PROSPECT FILE

The prospect-file cards should be well planned. They should have room for as much relevant information concerning each prospect as possible. A family or residence card may contain the names of several individuals depending on the number in the family. An estimate of each prospect's age should be entered and each should be designated as prospect for baptism, transfer or re-commitment of life.

The file card ought to be larger than the survey card so that there will be ample room for the callers to write in the results of the last call made. There can be four or more spaces for these entries, especially if the back of the card is utilized. Each entry should be dated with the day, month and year of the call. The file card may be five by eight inches high. Standard file boxes are obtainable in this size. See Chapter Five for a sample of both the front and the back of a file card.

Keeping the prospect file in order and up to date is of necessity time-consuming. However, this time so spent is vital to the evangelism program. Unless there is a chairman of evangelism on hand to work the file faithfully, the minister himself had better tackle it. If the job is delegated to someone else, the volunteer must be completely dedicated and well-trained for this important job.

The prospect file box may be divided into two main sections with a center divider. Alphabetical tabs may be used in the back section, with area-designating tabs in the front. These front tabs divide the city into north, east, south, west, downtown area, across the river, etc. The cards may be moved from back to front (from the alphabetical section to the area section) for the purpose of assignment of calls. It makes good sense to assign the calls by area, so that there can be more calling time and less driving time expended on any given calling night.

Entries should be made on the cards after the calls are completed, and then the cards are returned to the alphabetical section of the file. The file should be searched each week for the better prospects so that these cards may be placed to the front for assignment. New prospect names should be coming in weekly. Most of these new cards will probably begin at the front of the file, since newer prospects are usually the most urgent.

## THE TRAINING/WITNESSING PROGRAM

On the last Sunday before the starting date of the program we have a consecration service for the workers. This is usually done after the invitation hymn and before the benediction. We call the trainers and trainees to the front. We announce to the congregation that these people, both trainers and trainees, are enlisted for a four month tour of duty. We offer a prayer of dedication for them and then enlist the congregation for prayer during the entire period.

Training sessions are held regularly each week. In our local church, the sessions are held on Tuesday nights from 7:00 till 9:30, Wednesday mornings from 9:30 till noon and, for youth

Thursday afternoons from 3:30 till 6:00. The first half-hour of each session is devoted to the classroom study of the Gospel outline and of the best methods of witnessing. The remaining two hours are spent in visitation.

Trainers and trainees must be firmly committed to the two and one-half hours per week for personal evangelism during the four month tour. If there are three sessions per week, any given trainee or trainer need only attend one of them.

A three-session week is a realistic plan. For a slower start into the program a church may have only one or two sessions weekly. However, we heard of one preacher who had five weekly sessions because of his desire to produce several trainers in a short time. This would seem to be too heavy a pace for the average person.

Generally, it is best to begin fairly small. The preacher may be the only trainer. He can take out two persons as trainees. This should triple the number of trainers for the next four month period.

By all means, a nursery should be provided on calling nights. This opens the door to both husband and wife being in the program.

Attendance to sessions is vitally important. And since the class is only for one half-hour, being on time is essential. It is well to set the time of arrival at 6:55, and then see that the preacher starts the class at exactly 7:00 P.M. - - not even 30 seconds late.

An attendance chart is plotted on a large white display board made of a stiff paper substance. The chart is blocked off into squares with horizontal and vertical lines. There should be a vertical column for each date of the program period. Names of workers are entered at the left, in line with the horizontal lines of the chart. If there are seventeen sessions during the tour, each name has seventeen blocks after it. We have three rubber stamps for these blocks - - a star, a devil and a capital "E". The star is for present, the devil is for absent and the "E" means excused for reasons given in advance. No excuses are accepted after the absence. A rubber stamp concern can make these stamps. A red pad is used for the devil stamp. Three devils means that one is out of the program for that round. See Chapter Five for a chart sample and rubber stamp images. You may trace the devil and star image out of this book for the rubber stamp ordering.

## THE CLASS TIME

The half-hour class session can begin with a song and prayer. The preacher is the instructor for this short class period in which the presentation of the Gospel plan of salvation is studied.

An outline is taught which provides the caller with a definite track to run on. A simple Christ-centered presentation is dealt with in Chapter Four.

During the thirty minute class period we work on the memorization of the Gospel outline and of the supporting Scriptural references. Each week we assign "homework" of certain sections and of passages to be memorized. Although we encourage everyone to memorize the outline, we caution them against making a presentation sound "canned." After the material has been memorized and digested, each worker is encouraged to learn to present it in a natural way, using his own personality and language.

As the training approaches the half-way point we begin to deal with the problem of answering the excuses and overcoming the obstacles which are often encountered in personal evangelism. In our class sessions we begin having sample presentations. Some of the trainers are asked to play the role of typical prospects We ask them to be neither too easy nor too hard to "convert." Before the four month period is completed, every trainee should have staged a sample Gospel presentation to one of the trainers. This is a requirement for graduation.

At the final session during the training period a written examination is given. Mainly, it involves the writing of the outline and of the supporting Scriptures. A Sunday night graduation follows at which time certificates are awarded. See Chapter Five for a sample certificate.


## THE CALLING TIME

We end the class time and begin the calling time each week with a few sentence prayers. We must rely upon the power of the Holy Spirit to guide us in the important challenge of witnessing. We can say "Amen" to the prayer of one young lady who during this prayer time petitioned: "Lord, deliver us from the folly of our own wisdom, and lead us with Thy Holy Spirit as we go out to witness."

Preparation for calling must be made before the actual calling time. Assignment cards with the names and addresses of prospects have already been stacked in groups and each team is given about four calls to make. These are probably more than will be needed, but it does allow for the ever present problem of not finding people at home. It should be decided ahead of time which stack goes to which trainer-trainee team.

Another advance assignment for the preacher and/or the evangelism chairman involves the matter of teaming up the workers. Two trainees are teamed with one trainer. We believe it is wise to rotate the team combinations rather than keeping the same trios together each week, because trainees can learn more by observing different trainers and thus can feel their way into their own personal style of presenting the Gospel. Since rotation is weekly, the matter of teaming up the workers must be tended to on the planning sheet beforehand. This is a must because of time limitation - - both the assignments of calls and the establishment of calling teams must be planned ahead of time.

One of the first questions that a reader will ask is, "Why three to a calling team?" In considering this we should remember that a trainer is training others. The trainers include both men and women. It would not be discreet for a man trainer to train another man's wife in a two by two calling program. Jesus did not have this problem when sending out His disciples by twos, because they were all men. If all of our callers were men, the two by two plan would be fine. The three by three approach allows a man to call with anybody's wife or sweetheart without the taint of indiscretion. He can train on any given night a man and a woman or two women. Another notable advantage is that more people can be trained in a given period of time. In three years we have never had any problem arise from the fact that we appeared at the home in teams of three rather than two.

Two things should be avoided, however. (1) Three men should not be grouped together. Often only the woman of the house is at home. Three men on a porch would probably alarm the average housewife answering her door-bell. It is permissable, however, for three women to be teamed up if one of them is the trainer. (2) Husband and wife should not be teamed together. If this is done, the third party in the calling trio might feel out of place, like an extra thumb on a hand. Also each trainee is a prospective trainer, which means that a husband and wife team would have to be separated after the training period. This change in pace could weaken their effectiveness as trainers.

The transition from the half-hour in class to the two hours of calling must be expedited. The half-hour ends with sentence prayers. The teams can go out immediately if the teaming of workers and assignment of cards has already been worked out. Gospel tracts, church brochures, decision cards and other helpful materials should be made readily available as well as a good supply of city maps. Callers are urged to plot their route before going to their cars. This saves time in the long run. Each caller carries with him a pocket size New Testament. Every car has a flashlight for finding house numbers.

We cannot over-emphasize the Spiritual aspect of the calling. Each team of three should have still another prayer for their particular calls. This is best done in the car before starting the engine. Each should pray earnestly for God's guidance and for

His intervention in encouraging the prospects to be receptive to the Gospel.

As a team of three enters a home to present the Gospel, each member of the calling party exchanges friendly greetings with the people of the house. The trainer, however, is the one who carries the ball in the actual witnessing. Trainees need not remain mute during this time. This could appear unnatural in the eyes of the prospect. They can add a brief word here and there during the Gospel presentation, but they should allow the trainer to proceed with the witnessing and in the seeking for a decision. Often trainees can aid in helping with a small child who is interfering with the witnessing endeavor.

The subject matter employed in the call is Christ-centered. It deals with the Bible-revealed plan of salvation and aims toward a definite decision for Christ.

After two months in the program, trainees begin to take part in the presentation. During the fourth month trainees may begin making the entire presentation. Such a teaching-learning procedure is in keeping with human nature itself. Academic learning is not enough. Experience is indeed the best teacher. Trainees learn to witness in an observation-participation program. Observation gives way to participation not abruptly, but gradually, over the four month period of time. Prospective recruits for evangelism need not hesitate on the basis of not knowing how, or because of being afraid to witness. The very nature of this program wipes out these excuses. A learner is not under pressure; he or she starts out as little more than an observer. The trainer is there to carry the ball. This selling point should be used in recruitment.

By the completion of the four month training period every trainee should have made at least one presentation in a home, probably more than one. Also he will have made a model presentation during the class period and will have taken the final written examination on the Gospel outline. He should now be ready to assume the role of trainer for the next training period.


## MAKING THE PROGRAM PERMANENT

Ministers and congregations have entered into this sort of evangelism training program with great enthusiasm. Often the program thrives for several months. However, there will come the inevitable periods of discouragement. The minister and his people may be ready to abandon it as just another church program that worked at least for a while. Nothing could make Satan happier than to see an evangelism endeavor forsaken. If there is any church activity, aside from regular worship, which needs to be a permanent part of church life, indeed it is evangelism.

It should be an evangelism involving as much of the total church as possible.

Church people have grown accustomed to working with planned calendar events. We have our "times and seasons." The time comes for pre-Easter planning; a time comes for Vacation Bible School planning; a time comes for the preparation of Thanksgiving and Christmas programs, choir cantatas, etc. The financial year with its budget and faith commitment requires intensive preparation, as does the yearly revival. Likewise, it is imperative to make the evangelism training program a year-round church habit. If we have a great four months we praise the Lord. If we have a disappointing round, we pray even harder for a better one next time. This is the same philosophy that a church has concerning its yearly revival. If we have a weak one this year, we try harder for success next year.

In short, we would say, "Keep the evangelism training program alive." Make "Restoring First Century Evangelism" a permanent part of church life. It should never be treated as a one-time experimental program which is doomed to lose its identity among other programs. It should never be crowded out by other entities in church life. It should be kept vividly before the people. The cycle of two months of preparation and four months of training in evangelism, occuring twice yearly, should be built into the total church life, and as such should hold a prominent place in the eyes of the people.

There may come a time when the program seems to reach a "saturation point" - - a time when there are more than enough trainers for the number of trainees who have been recruited for the next round. Do not let the program die or bog down at this point. The trainers can team together and continue to call and to train those new recruits who are willing to learn. Also some of the leaders in neighboring churches, who might be interested in starting such a program in their own churches, might like to sign up as trainees. Even though there will be the inevitable times of discouragement, there will always be those who are willing to be used by the Lord in the great venture of soul-winning. Pray that the Lord will continue to send laborers into the vineyard. Evangelism is the first business of the church!

*CHAPTER FOUR*

## THE GOSPEL PRESENTED

Having considered the mechanics of the program for "Restoring First Century Evangelism," let us now consider the way in which the Gospel is actually presented to an individual. This chapter is devoted chiefly to the challenge of witnessing to a non-Christian, but we will also note the approach to make to a baptized person who does not have local church membership and to an immersed backslider who may or may not have his name on a local church register.

## WITNESSING TO THE LOST

The team of callers, after seeking God's guidance in prayer, will be able to knock confidently on the prospect's door. This confidence is available to all, for Jesus said, "Lo, I am with you" (Matthew 28:20). The approach at the door is made with poise, accompanied by a warm friendly smile. The hand-shake also is friendly and confident, striking the pleasant medium between the "deadfish" and the "bone-crusher" grip. It is very important to be pleasant and smiling with an easy, winsome and relaxed bearing; the Gospel cannot be shared in a tense atmosphere. Pharasaical smugness will surely turn people off fast.

The presentation is made in stages with a kind of "gear-shifting" operation. Try to stay on the subject, avoid side-tracking and at the same time make smooth transitions from the casual to the serious. (1) "Low gear" can represent the initial small talk. This will wear thin if it lasts for more than three or four minutes. In the back of the prospect's mind will be the question, "What did you come here to say?" (2) A "second gear" transition can involve questions about the prospect's church background and some good remarks about your local church and its program. (3) The "high gear" transition takes us into the actual presentation of the Gospel. This can be accomplished by a serious question or two about the prospect's personal salvation; for example: "Have you come to the Spiritual satisfaction of knowing for certain that if Jesus would return today, He would take you with Him to heaven?" This general thought can be expressed in various ways. How the prospect answers is not the important thing. The point is that we have made the transition. After shifting to the subject of the Gospel plan of salvation, every effort should be made to avoid side-tracking.

There are seven main topics that must be covered thoroughly and clearly when presenting the Gospel to an individual. They are:

        I.    MAN
        II.   GOD
        III.  GRACE
        IV.   JESUS CHRIST
        V.    FAITH
        VI.   OBEDIENCE
        VII.  ASSURANCE

The following is a general outline of a presentation in which the analogy of a flight is used:


## RESTORING FIRST CENTURY EVANGELISM
*Person To Person Presentation Of The Gospel*

**I.  THE TAKE OFF**
  A.  Very, very brief "small talk" warm-up.  Introductions — warm, friendly encounter.
  B.  Ask about prospect's family, job, hometown, etc. Keep it short.  Avoid long parlor conversation.
  C.  *FIRST TRANSITION.* Start first stage of transition in the conversation by asking about prospect's church background.

**II.  THE FLIGHT BEGINS**
  A.  Now talk about the local church and the program it offers.
  B.  In just three or four short sentences tell about the Bible church doctrinal plea — "We strive to follow the Bible only," "We seek to restore the church of the first century," etc. ........................ *Matthew 16:18  Acts 2:47*
  C.  Give a short personal testimony as to what Christ means to you.  This eases you into the second transition.
  D.  *SECOND TRANSITION.* Prepare to shift the conversation to the next vitally important stage — the prospect's personal salvation.  The transition accomplished, don't lose it.  Avoid sidetracking.
  E.  Two lead-in questions (the first of five very important questions in this outline.  The last three are near the end.)
      QUESTION NUMBER 1: "Have you come to the place in your life where you can say for sure that if Jesus were to return today, He would take you to heaven with Him?"
      .................... *I John 5:13*
      QUESTION NUMBER 2: "If you were to die this very day, and God would ask you: 'Why should I give you eternal life,' how would you reply?" ......... *Matthew 5:48*

      *(Regardless of answers the conversation has shifted to*

*the right level.)*

### III. THE FLIGHT ESTABLISHES ITS COURSE AS WE PRESENT THE GOSPEL AND ITS PLAN OF SALVATION

A. MAN's condition (presenting need of plan of salvation must precede the plan itself.)
1. All men are sinners. ...........*Romans 6:23   Romans 3:23*
2. Man cannot save himself. ......................*Proverbs 14:12*

B. GOD'S NATURE
1. GOD loves us and does not want us to go to hell.
....................*Jeremiah 31:3   John 3:16*
2. But since God is also a just God, punishment for sin is a just necessity. ..................*Exodus 34:7   Psalms 89:32*

C. Therefore man can only be saved by GRACE. Grace means 'unearned favor' . . . God gives the plan of salvation and heaven by His Grace.
.................... *Acts 15:11   Titus 3:5   Ephesians 2:8-9*

D. JESUS CHRIST Brings Grace
1. Who He is. He is God's Son who came in the flesh.
....................*John 1:14   Matthew 16:16*
2. He established His church. ...*Matthew 16:18   Acts 2:47*
3. He came to save you by Grace.
   (a). He died for our sins, and He arose.
   (b). He took our place in punishment on the cross. Hence we can be saved in harmony with both God's love and justice. ...*Isaiah 53:5,6   I John 1:7   I Peter 2:24*
   *Romans 5:8   John 3:16*

E. God has done His part. NOW, what must I do to be saved? Heaven cannot be earned. It is a free gift which may be received by:
1. FAITH
   (a). Faith is not a mere belief in the head that Jesus is Christ.................................................... *James 2:19*
   (b). Faith is giving yourself completely to Jesus for salvation. Cease trusting self and start trusting Christ ..........................*Hebrews 11:1   Acts 16:31,33* Heaven is a free gift which may be received by Faith and . . .
2. OBEDIENCE. Obedience includes:
   (a). Accepting Jesus as your Lord, as God's Son.
   ..........................*Mark 16:16*
   (b). Repentance from sin. ..............................*Luke 13:3*
   (c). Open confession of your belief in Christ.
   ....................*Matthew 10:32*
   (d). Bible - taught baptism as immersion into Christ.
   *John 3:5   Acts 2:38   Romans 6:3,4   Galatians 3:27*

**(e).** Relying on Jesus to help you stay faithful.

*.................... Revelation 2:10*

**(f).** Now, hold your Bible open to the account of the conversion of the man from Ethiopia..... *Acts 8:26-39*
*Go over it with the prospect. Also you can show that Jesus set the example for immersion.... Matthew 3:13-17*

## IV. THE LANDING — SECURING THE DECISION

**A.** *THIRD TRANSITION.* Leads to the actual commitment. QUESTION NUMBER 3: (This is the lead-in question. Ask it after presenting the plan of salvation above. It leads into a decision).

"DOES THIS MAKE SENSE?" Most prospects will answer "yes."

**B.** The actual questions follow:
QUESTION NUMBER 4: "Are you willing to trust the Lord Jesus Christ to save you?" *..................... John 14:15*
QUESTION NUMBER 5: "Are you willing to obey Him?"

*.......................... Acts 2:38; Mark 16:16*

**C.** Clarify the decision - use decision card dated Sunday or sooner. Request name of prospect affixed to card.

**D.** ASSURANCE that Jesus will save. *................. I John 5:13*
Prayer of commitment.
Thanksgiving and rejoicing.

This outline of the presentation of the Gospel puts the caller in touch with something definite to aim toward when making personal evangelism calls. Too often in the past our careless procedures have caused us to make totally impromptu calls. Often we would have no idea of what we were planning to say as we approached a prospect's door. Consequently, we would do little more than drop a casual invitation to come pay a visit to church.

Of course, a first necessity in effective personal evangelism is to be totally assured of our own salvation in Christ. The Scriptures used in this Gospel presentation impart to us this blessed assurance that we are saved. When we have this assurance we are ready to share it with others.

The average church member, if he or she is truly born again in Jesus, can witness to and win others to Christ. However, the willing Christian must be taught to do so. The outline should become a part of each and every caller. This is accomplished by (1) memorizing it, (2) absorbing its content to the point that the Gospel message is as much in his mind as his own name and address and (3) practicing it regularly in the vital activity of personal evangelism. Consequently, the message of the Gospel outline will be much more than something memorized; it will become a living, vital message to employ in bringing precious souls to Christ.

## SOME STUDY GUIDES AND HELPS

On the following pages are some materials which we have used successfully in helping our callers learn to present the Gospel effectively. The first is a diagram that relates various Scripture references to the different parts of the Gospel outline. We cannot emphasize enough the importance of keeping the Bible references central in presenting the Gospel. Herein we witness the power behind the wonderful message of redemption. The caller should establish every point by Scripture. Let the Word of God speak in all its persuasive power. Use the diagram as an aid in the memorization of the Scripture verses so vital to effective personal evangelism.

## Left column verses

On this rock I will build my church, and the gates of Hades will not overcome it.
*Matthew 16:18*

And the Lord added to their number daily those who were being saved.
*Acts 2:47*

I write these things . . . so that you may know that you have eternal life.
*1 John 5:13*

The wages of sin is death, but the gift of God is eternal life through Christ Jesus our Lord.
*Romans 6:23*

All have sinned and fall short of the glory of God.
*Romans 3:23*

There is a way which seems right to a man, but its end is the way of death.
*Proverbs 14:12*

[God] will by no means leave the guilty unpunished.
*Exodus 34:7*

Then I will visit their transgression with the rod, and their iniquity with stripes.
*Psalm 89:32*

I have loved you with an everlasting love.
*Jeremiah 31:3*

For God so loved the world that he gave his one and only Son, that whoever believes in him shall not perish but have everlasting life.
*John 3:16*

We believe it is through the grace of our Lord Jesus that we are saved.
*Acts 15:11*

He saved us, not because of righteous things we had done, but because of his mercy.
*Titus 3:5*

By grace you have been saved, through faith—and this not from yourselves, it is the gift of God —not by works, so that no one can boast.
*Ephesians 2:8, 9*

The Word became flesh and lived for a while among us. We have seen his glory, the glory of the one and only Son, who came from the Father, full of grace and truth.
*John 1:14*

You are the Christ, the Son of the living God.
*Matthew 16:16*

He was pierced through for our transgressions, He was crushed for our iniquities . . . All of us like sheep have gone astray, each of us has turned to his own way; but the Lord has caused the iniquity of us all to fall on Him.
*Isaiah 53:5, 6*

## Center outline

# OUTLINE IN BRIEF AS A LEARNING AID

**I. The Take Off**
   A. Brief friendly warm up
   B. Hometown, etc.
   C. Church background. Transition

**II. The Flight Begins**
   A. Our local church. Doctrine
   B. Personal testimony
   C. Important questions: One and Two

**III. Flight Continues— Gospel Presented**
   A. Man
      1. A sinner
      2. Cannot save self
   B. God
      1. Justice
      2. Love
   C. Grace
   D. Jesus
      1. God's Son
      2. What He did to save us
   E. Plan of Salvation
      1. Faith
      2. Obedience
         a. Repentance
         b. Confession of Christ
         c. Baptism
         d. Faithfulness

**IV. The Landing**
   A. A qualifying question
   B. Conversion of the Ethiopian
   C. The TWO decision questions
   D. Clarification
   E. Prayer

**V. Assurance**
   1 John 5:13

They devoted themselves to the apostles' teaching and to the fellowship, to the breaking of bread and to prayer. *Acts 2:42*

Let us not give up meeting together, as some are in the habit of doing, but let us encourage one another—and all the more as you see the Day approaching. If we deliberately keep on sinning after we have received the knowledge of the truth, no sacrifice for sins is left.
*Hebrews 10:25, 26*

All Old Testament Scriptures are taken from the *New American Standard Bible,* © The Lockman Foundation, 1963.

All New Testament Scriptures are taken from the *The New International Version of the New Testament,* © 1973 by New York Bible Society International. Used by permission.

## Right column verses

The blood of Jesus, his Son, purifies us from every sin.
*1 John 1:7*

He himself bore our sins in his body on the cross . . . by his wounds you have been healed.
*1 Peter 2:24*

God demonstrates his own love for us in this: While we were still sinners, Christ died for us.
*Romans 5:8*

You believe that there is one God. Good! Even the demons believe that—and shudder.
*James 2:19*

Now faith is being sure of what we hope for and certain of what we do not see. *Hebrews 11:1*

Believe in the Lord Jesus, and you will be saved . . . At that hour of the night the jailer took them and washed their wounds; then immediately he and all his family were baptized.
*Acts 16:31, 33*

Whoever believes and is baptized will be saved, but whoever does not believe will be condemned. *Mark 16:16*

Unless you repent, you too will all perish. *Luke 13:3*

Whoever acknowledges me before men, I will also acknowledge him before my Father in heaven. *Matthew 10:32*

Unless a man is born of water and the Spirit, he cannot enter the kingdom of God. *John 3:5*

Repent and be baptized, every one of you, in the name of Jesus Christ so that your sins may be forgiven. And you will receive the gift of the Holy Spirit.
*Acts 2:38*

Don't you know that all of us who were baptized into Christ Jesus were baptized into his death? We were therefore buried with him through baptism into death in order that, just as Christ was raised from the dead through the glory of the Father, we too may live a new life.
*Romans 6:3, 4*

All of you who were united with Christ in baptism have been clothed with Christ.
*Galatians 3:27*

Be faithful, even to the point of death, and I will give you the crown of life. *Revelation 2:10*

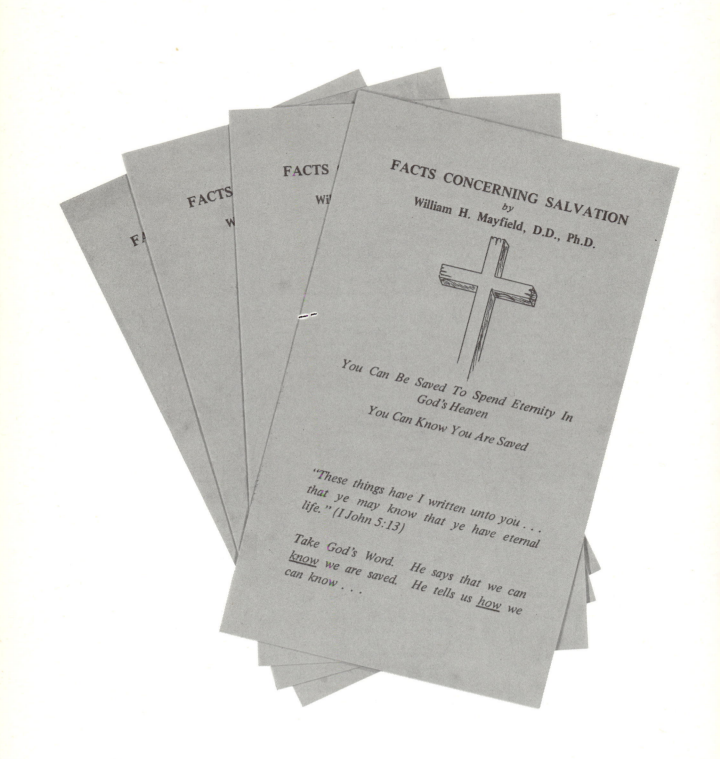

FACTS CONCERNING SALVATION
*by*
William H. Mayfield, D.D., Ph.D.

You Can Be Saved To Spend Eternity In
God's Heaven

You Can Know You Are Saved

"These things have I written unto you . . .
that ye may know that ye have eternal
life." (1 John 5:13)

Take God's Word. He says that we can
know we are saved. He tells us *how* we
can know . . .

*YOU CAN BE SAVED and*
*YOU CAN KNOW YOU ARE SAVED*

## Outline Of Gospel In Brief

**MAN** — In God's image but lost.

"FOR THE WAGES OF SIN IS DEATH; but the gift of God is eternal life through Jesus Christ our Lord."

*Romans 6:23*

"For all have sinned and come short of the glory of God."

*Romans 3:23*

**GOD** — He loves us - *John 3:16,* but sin must be punished.

"God will by no means clear the guilty."          *Exodus 34:7*

**GRACE** — Free Gift of Salvation which we cannot earn.

"But we believe that through the grace of the Lord Jesus Christ we shall be saved."          *Acts 15:11*

**JESUS** — He brings God's Grace to us.

"The blood of Jesus Christ cleanseth us from all sin."

*I John 1:7*

"Who His own self bare our sins in His own body on the tree . . . by whose stripes we are healed."          *I Peter 2:24*

**FAITH** — More than head belief - Faith is trust in Christ for salvation.

"Thou believest that there is one God; thou doest well: the devils also believed, and trembled."          *James 2:19*

"Faith is the substance of things hoped for, and the evidence of things not seen."          *Hebrews 11:1*

**OBEDIENCE** — Salvation is a free gift from God which we can receive by faith and obedience.

"He that believeth and is baptized shall be saved; and he that believeth not shall be damned."          *Mark 16:16*

**ASSURANCE** — You can know you are saved.

"These things have I written unto you . . . that ye may know that ye have eternal life."          *I John 5:13*

**ASSURANCE FOR ETERNITY** — "Be thou faithful unto death, and I will give thee a crown of life."          *Revelation 2:10*

*NOW, MAY WE CONSIDER TOGETHER THIS GOSPEL OUTLINE WHICH WE HAVE TAKEN FROM GOD'S WORD?*

**MAN** — *Genesis 1:27* tells us that we are made in God's image. We disgraced this God-like image when we sinned. The result of sin was damnation. "For the wages of sin is death . . ." *(Romans 6:23).* Everybody has sinned - "For all have sinned . . ." *(Romans 3:23).* This includes me. Hence we all appear before God in a very bad light. In view of this to whom can we turn for help? To whom but . . . .

**GOD** — "God is LOVE" *(I John 4:8)*. Because God loves us He does not want us to go to hell. God is "not willing that any should perish, but that all should come to repentance." *(II Peter 3:9)*.

However, God by His very nature is also a God of JUSTICE. Therefore, sin must be punished. God "will by no means clear the guilty." *(Exodus 34:7)*. Also, "Then will I visit their transgressions with the rod and their iniquities with stripes." *(Psalm 89:32)*.

This makes our lost condition seem even more hopeless. If you have been to court and have lost the trial, and you are awaiting the judge to pronounce sentence, you have only one last appeal. You can cry out to the judge for MERCY. This is exactly where we stand with God.

**GRACE** — Mercy is an act of GRACE. Grace means an "unearned gift." We could earn eternal life by being perfect. Jesus said, "Be ye perfect even as your Father which is in heaven is perfect." *(Matthew 5:48)*. However, none of us qualifies on this basis. Therefore, we can be saved ONLY by God's GRACE - a gift given to us in spite of the fact that we do not deserve it.

"By grace are ye saved through faith." *(Ephesians 2:8)*.

But, we have just said that God is JUST and sin MUST be punished. How, then, can He give us grace? This is where JESUS CHRIST comes into the picture.

**JESUS** — He "bore our sins in His own body on the tree . . . by His stripes we are healed." *(I Peter 2:24)*. Hence, our sin IS punished; only Jesus is willing to bear our punishment in our place on the cross. So then, God's law of justice is not violated. Jesus died and arose to take away the guilt of our sins.

"God shows His love toward us, in that while we were yet sinners, Christ died for us." *(Romans 5:8)*.

He is the only Begotten Son of God *(Matthew 16:16)*. He is God who became man *(John 1:1,14)*. Because this is true, He can save us. He did so on the cross. "The blood of Jesus Christ cleanseth us from all sin." *(I John 1:7)*.

**FAITH** — Therefore, heaven is a free gift which you can receive by FAITH in Jesus Christ and by OBEDIENCE to Him.

Faith is not just head-belief. The devil also "believed and trembled." *(James 2:19)*. For example, you believe Napoleon lived, but you don't trust him to do anything for you. Even an unrepenting drunkard can say that he believes in Jesus.

However, belief, plus TRUST in Jesus to save, equals faith. You can begin to have faith when you add this TRUST to your head-belief.

**OBEDIENCE** —

1. Having FAITH which TRUSTS Jesus to save, we will obey Him if we really have such a faith.

2. Jesus commands REPENTANCE. He says that if we do not repent we will perish. *(Luke 13:3)*. Repentance means the act of turning over our whole life to Jesus Christ, withholding no part of ourselves from Him.

3. Repentance will lead to open CONFESSION of our faith in Jesus. Jesus said to confess Him before men *(Matthew 10:32)*. If we do this, He will confess us before God.

4. God's Word commands BAPTISM. From the original Greek, the word is BAPTIZO which means "immerse." Jesus said, "He that believeth and is baptized shall be saved." *(Mark 16:16)*.

   Baptism is commanded, " . . . Repent and be baptized every one of you, in the name of Jesus Christ for the remission of sins, and ye shall receive the gift of the Holy Spirit." *(Acts 2:38)*.

   This verse tells us that with baptism we receive:

   (1)  Forgiveness of sins (in Christ) and

   (2)  God  the Holy Spirit in us.

   *Romans 6:4* tells us that baptism is a burial and a resurrection. Only immersion captures this picture.

**ASSURANCE**  —  By  FAITH  in Christ alone to save, and by OBEDIENCE,  you can know you have received God's grace. "For as many of you as have been baptized into Christ have put on Christ." *(Galatians 3:27)*.

"These things have I written unto you that believe on the name of the Son of God; that ye may know that ye have eternal life, and that ye may believe on the name of the Son of God." *(I John 5:13)*.

**ASSURANCE FOR ETERNITY**  —  *Revelation 2:10* commands us to be faithful unto death to be eternally saved.  How do we remain faithful unto death?  In Acts 2:42 we have a one verse formula for staying saved forever.  It says, "And they continued steadfastly in the APOSTLES' DOCTRINE, and FELLOWSHIP,  and in BREAKING OF BREAD, and in PRAYERS."  *(Acts 2:42)*.  If you do these things after baptism, you will never fall from God's saving grace.

Continue faithfully in:

(1)  APOSTLES' DOCTRINE  —  A Christian should study the Bible, both the New Testament and the Old Testament, every day.  Be sure your daily Bible reading includes the New Testament. *(II Timothy 2:15)*.

(2)  FELLOWSHIP  —  Worship with the people of God regularly. *Hebrews 10:25* says not to neglect it. Even one worship service missed is a step toward backsliding.

(3) BREAKING OF BREAD — Weekly observance of the communion is necessary. *John 6:53* teaches us that we are spiritually dead without it. *Acts 20:7* infers that the early church communed weekly.

(4) PRAYER — A Christian should begin and end the day with prayer and should pray often every day. *(I Thessalonians 5:17)*.

These four things will keep you saved forever and will keep you growing as a Christian. Your growth should lead you into witnessing to others about Christ.

The presentation in this tract can help you do just that.

THE CHURCH — We are baptized into Christ, not into a church, but "The Lord adds to the Church all that are saved." *(Acts 2:47)*.

There is only one church in the Bible. It is neither Protestant nor Catholic. It is Christ's Church and wears His name. We are dedicated to restoring the Spirit of the first century church. Read about the one church in *Matthew 16:18, John 17:21, Ephesians 4:4-5, Acts 4:12,* etc. Read of its origin in *Acts, chapter 2.*

In joining Christ, you do not join a denomination, you are added to Christ's Church. The Christian churches and churches of Christ are dedicated to these principles.

MAY GOD BLESS YOU AND LEAD YOU TO ETERNAL LIFE.

"These things have I written unto you that believe on the Son of God; that ye may know that ye have eternal life." *(I John 5:13).*

Tract prepared by Dr. William H. Mayfield. Available from Standard Publishing (order # 3251).

## PERSON TO PERSON WITNESSING
### A Sample Presentation

We would like at this point to bring the preceding materials and suggestions together into a sample Gospel presentation to lost persons. Of course, no two presentations will be exactly alike. The way in which the prospect reacts helps to guide us in employing the best elements of the outline to use at any given time. But in general an evangelistic call might be very similar to this sample presentation which involves trainer Bill Smith, trainees Jane Doe and John Jones and prospects Don and Ann Martin on whom the trio is calling. (The names and places used here are fictitious and refer to no persons living or dead.)

After prayer, the calling team drives to the home of Mr. and Mrs. Don Martin. The door bell rings and is answered by Ann Martin. Trainer Bill will be doing most of the talking.

"Good evening! You are Mrs. Martin, I believe!"

"Yes."

"I'm Bill Smith, a member of the First Christian Church. We're engaged in some church calling this evening. I have with me Jane Doe and John Jones. May we visit with you for a little while?"

"Yes, come in."

"Thank you so much!"

"This is my husband, Don."

Handshaking and acknowledgment of introductions proceed in a conventional way. Bill tries to seat himself in a position where he can talk conveniently with both Don and Ann Martin. Trainees help accomplish this by taking the more distant seats. The callers will soon learn that Don has been immersed, but has for years been an inactive member of a denominational church located some fifty miles away. Ann has never made a decision for Christ. Bill Smith continues:

"You folk have a lovely home. Have you lived here long?"

"Nearly ten years now," replies Don.

"Do either of you have local church membership?"

"I used to be a member of a Baptist church over near Bright Springs, but I haven't been active for a long time," answers Don.

"I presume then that you have been immersed?"

"Yes, I was baptized in Big Stone Creek on a cold day in December."

"You will never forget that, will you?"

"No, Sir!"

"And you, Mrs. Martin?"

"I have never joined a church."

"Is it all right if we call you by your first names?"

"Please do!"

"Thank you! You have probably visited our services at First

Christian, haven't you?"

"We have been planning to but, sorry to say, we haven't yet. How did you know about us?"

"Psychic, I guess. No, I believe it was through our church survey."

"I see."

"We have what we feel to be the friendliest church in town; at least we are trying to be. We maintain a full program for youth and for all ages. Do you have children?"

"We have one nine year old boy. He is at Cub meeting this evening."

"Fine! What pack is he in?"

"At the fire hall."

"Very good! We have a lot of church activities for both children and youth. Have you heard much about the Christian churches and churches of Christ?"

"Not a lot."

"We are attempting to base our entire belief, as well as our activities, on the Bible alone. We have no man-written creeds. Our goal is to go back to the pattern of the church of the first century, New Testament period. Hence, we seek to be un-denominational - - just Christians. Does this sound reasonable to you?"

"Why, yes! That sounds right to me."

"Fine! We know that back there, two thousand years ago, Christ told of His coming church. In Matthew 16 we hear Him say, 'Upon this rock I will build my church,' and then we read in the book of Acts that 'the Lord added to the church all that were saved.' (Matthew 16:18 and Acts 2:47). This almost 2000 year old church is what we are striving to be at First Christian."

(NOTE: For the reader's benefit we put the exact Scripture references in parentheses. However, we do not recommend citing exact references by chapter and verse to the prospect. If we were to do this, it might distract from the Gospel message itself and it could also leave a "showing-off" impression. Hence, rather than to say, "Jesus says in Matthew 16:18 . . . ," we say something like, "In Matthew 16 we hear Him say . . . " or "We read in the book of Matthew how Jesus says . . . " However, we do keep the references in mind to cite if necessary.)

The Martins nod in apparent agreement.

Bill Smith continues, "Of course, I am a part of Christ's church only because He is willing to include me. Since I became a Christian, I have found a new life with Christ which provides me with greater personal peace and deeper happiness than I could ever have imagined. How wonderful to be a Christian!"

Jane Doe says, "Indeed it is!"

John Jones nods in agreement.

Bill Smith is smiling as he alternately looks both of the Martins in the eye. "The main reason we are out calling tonight is not to talk about our church but to speak a good word for Jesus. Don and Ann, please let me ask you a question about your own relationship with Jesus. Have you come to the place in your life that you know for certain that if Jesus were to return today, He would take you with Him to heaven?"

"I don't know. Can anyone know that for certain?"

"It would be hard for me to believe that anyone could be sure of his salvation if it were not for the fact that the Bible says we can. We read in the fifth chapter of John's first epistle, 'These things have I written unto you . . . that ye may know that you have eternal life.' (I John 5:13). Now, that is quite a promise, isn't it?"

"It certainly is!"

"Now, let's make the question even more personal - - if you were called from this life this very night, and found yourself standing before God and He were to ask you, 'Why should I give you eternal life,' what would you answer?"

Don replies, "I guess I'd just tell Him that I have done the best I could. I have tried to be decent and live by the Golden Rule."

"While striving toward the Golden Rule and the moral life is very admirable, can we really say that we have accomplished this goal? Jesus said in His Sermon on the Mount, 'Be ye perfect, even as your Father in heaven is perfect.' (Matthew 5:48). This is His requirement. But none of us has achieved this, have we?"

"No, I guess nobody is perfect."

"Then it is for certain that we will have to look to something other than our own goodness for salvation. Do you agree?"

"I suppose that is right."

"Now, let us see what our problem is. We will start right where we are, with man - - with all human beings. Who are we? Genesis tells us that we are created in God's image. However, we profaned His image when we sinned. In the book of Romans we read that 'all have sinned and come short of the glory of God' and that 'the wages of sin is death.' (Romans 3:23 and 6:23). In this context it means that the result of our sin is damnation. The book of Proverbs says that 'there is a way which seemeth right unto man, but the end thereof are the ways of death.' (Proverbs 14:12). Therefore, man just cannot save himself. He must look to a higher power. Now, if the result of sin is damnation, and if everyone has sinned, and if we can't save ourselves, this puts us all in a real bad light, doesn't it?"

"Yes, I guess it does."

"Now, in view of this terrible predicament, to whom can we turn for help?"

"Why, I guess to God."

"That is right. Let's see now if God can and will help us. Who is God? He is eternal, all powerful, all knowing and our Creator. The Bible tells us that 'God is love.' (I John 4:8). Through the prophet Jeremiah He said to us all, "I have loved thee with an everlasting love.' (Jeremiah 31:3). Therefore, because God loves us He does not want us to spend eternity in hell. Peter says, 'God is not willing that any should perish, but that all should come to repentance.' (II Peter 3:9). Isn't it great to know that God loves us?"

"It really is!"

"However, there is more to the nature of God. He is also a God of justice. According to the law of justice, sin must be punished. The Bible tells us, 'I will visit their transgressions with the rod and their iniquity with stripes.' (Psalm 89:32). Now, we recognize this principle as being valid. If I were to rob the local bank and in so doing kill someone and, as I am brought to trial, the judge would say to me, 'Bill, you did a terrible thing, but because I love you, I am going to turn you loose,' this would not make sense, would it?"

"No, it surely wouldn't."

"So you see, God cannot just turn us loose and still be a just and moral God. Sin has to be punished. Now, this puts us in even a worse light, doesn't it?"

"Yes, it does!"

"Here we are - - we have all sinned and sin must be punished. If I have been to court, and have lost the case, and the judge is preparing to pass sentence, there is only one last thing I can do. I can cry out to the judge for what?"

"Mercy."

"Yes! And this is exactly where we stand with God. Paul said that it is 'not by the works of righteousness which we have done but according to His mercy He saved us.' (Titus 3:5). Since we have not come up to the Lord's standard, 'Be ye perfect even as your Father in Heaven is perfect' (Matthew 5:48), His mercy is our only hope. Another Bible word for mercy is the term 'grace.' This means 'unearned favor.' Again Paul says, 'By grace are ye saved through faith; and that not of yourselves, it is the gift of God, not of works, lest any man should boast.' (Ephesians 2:8,9). Hence, God's grace, or mercy, is our only hope. But we still have a problem. We just pointed out Scripturally that God is just and, according to His law of justice, sin must be punished. In view of this, how can God give us His mercy?"

"It doesn't look like He can."

"Now, this is exactly where the Lord Jesus Christ comes into the picture. Who is Jesus? He is God who came to earth in the form of man. John says that He 'was made flesh, and dwelt among us and we beheld His glory, the glory of the only begotten of the

Father, full of grace and truth.' (John 1:14). Hence, God came bringing grace to save with Him. How did this happen? Isaiah prophesied, 'He was wounded for our transgressions, He was bruised for our iniquities . . . with His stripes we are healed.' (Isaiah 53:5). John said, 'The blood of Jesus Christ (shed on the cross) cleanseth us from all sin.' (I John 1:7). Peter said concerning Jesus, 'Who His own self bare our sins in His own body on the cross . . . by whose stripes we are healed.' (I Peter 2:24). Therefore, sin is punished. God does not violate His own law of justice. Jesus bore our punishment in our place when He died on the cross. He showed forth His power to do this when, after dying for us, He arose from the dead. Hence, 'God commendeth (showed) His love toward us, in that while we were yet sinners Christ died for us.' (Romans 5:8). The sinless Jesus bears our punishment for us, if we will let Him. Therefore, salvation in heaven is a free gift which God will give us if we will receive it on His terms. Those terms are faith and obedience. If a rich man were to write you a good check for ten-thousand dollars, it would be no good at all unless you were willing to cash it. Is this true?''

"Yes, that's right."

"Now, your willingness to receive the most generous gift ever offered, eternal life in heaven, is a 'must'! God will give you this gift if you accept it by faith and obedience. We can see that this is reasonable, can't we?''

"Yes."

"Let's ask then, What is faith? Faith is not just a belief in Jesus; it is much more. The book of James says, 'Thou believest that there is one God; thou doest well: the devils also believe and tremble.' (James 2:19). I suppose we could take an opinion poll of our entire community asking, 'Do you believe that Jesus is the Christ, God's only Son?' And ninety-five out of a hundred would answer, 'Yes.' You could ask the drunkard in the barroom the same question and there is a good chance that he would also answer, 'Yes.' This expression of a head-belief would not be a saving faith, would it?''

"No."

"What then is the difference between a belief in the head that will not save and a faith that will save? We can sum up the difference in one word, and that word is 'trust.' Are we willing to take a step beyond mere belief and trust Jesus all the way, on His terms to save us? This is the issue. If you were to go to the commercial airport to buy a ticket to New York, you would not walk up to the pilot and say, 'I demand to see your credentials, your pilot's license, log book, etc.' No, you would sit down, fasten your seat belt, and trust a man you had never seen with your very life. Jesus wants exactly this sort of trust on our part. The issue is, are we willing to trust Him all the way, and according to His way, to save us?  Belief plus trust equals faith.  Can you conceive His saving us otherwise?"

"I guess not."

"Now, if we have faith in Him, we certainly cannot refuse to obey Him.  You wouldn't get on that airliner we were talking about and say, 'I refuse to fasten my seat belt,' would you?"

"No, sir."

"Then to say we have faith in Jesus and, at the same time, refuse to obey Him would be even more unthinkable, wouldn't it?"

"I guess so."

"If we do what the Bible says, 'Believe on the Lord Jesus Christ,' (Acts 16:31) and we have the kind of faith defined in the book of Hebrews as 'the substance of things hoped for and the evidence of things not seen,' (Hebrews 11:1) we will then certainly want to obey what Jesus commands.  Do you agree?"

"Yes, that's right."

"If we trust Jesus, this means certainly that we love Him as well. Do you love Jesus, Who first loved you?"

"Why, yes."

"Jesus said, 'If ye love me, keep my commandments.' (John 14:15).  So this brings us face to face with obedience, doesn't it?"

"Yes."

"Let's see what obedience includes.  It includes the faith that we just discussed and it includes repentance  Jesus said, 'Except we repent, we shall perish.' (Luke 13:3).  Do you folk feel that you understand what the term 'repentance' means?"

"I believe we do.  Doesn't it mean that we are sorry for doing wrong?"

"That is at least part of it.  Paul said, 'Godly sorrow worketh repentance to salvation.' (II Corinthians 7:10).  The word from the original Bible Greek implies both to be sorry and to turn away from the world unto God.  The word carries the idea of turning - - a change of direction and a total change of purpose, from self and world to God.  It implies both the acts of changing the mind and turning.  Such a change will definitely point us to Christ.  Do you agree?"

"Certainly."

"Obedience also includes an open confession of our faith in Christ.  Jesus said, 'Whosoever shall confess Me before men, him will I confess also before my Father which is in heaven.' (Matthew 10:32).  A true follower of Jesus will not try to be such in secret. He will gladly confess his faith in the Lord not once but many times and at every opportunity.  Isn't the statement, 'I believe that Jesus is the Christ, the Son of God,' when said from the heart, the most important utterance we will ever make?"

"It must be."

"We note also in the Bible that we are commanded to be baptized. You say you were immersed into Christ, Don. Are you satisfied with your baptism?"

"Yes, I just haven't followed through like I should have."

"Even as his father received the prodigal son back with love, God is willing to receive you, if you make a full recommitment to Jesus. Let me ask, when you were baptized, Don, did you feel that your baptism was into Jesus, rather than into a church?"

"Yes, definitely."

"Fine. Now, Ann, have you at one time made a profession of faith and been baptized?"

"No, I never have."

"Perhaps we can look further now into the Word of God concerning this part of His plan of salvation. We find that baptism is a command. Jesus said that we must be 'born again' in order to reach heaven. Are you familiar with the expression, 'born again'?"

"I think so."

"He went on to say, 'Except one be born of water and of the Spirit, he cannot enter the kingdom of God.' (John 3:5). We read the command to be baptized in Acts, for example. Many of the people who had demanded Jesus' crucifixion were on hand in Jerusalem for the annual feast of Pentecost. Peter preached to them and convinced many of them that the man whom they had crucified had arisen, and indeed is the Christ. They were 'pricked in their hearts' and they asked, 'What shall we do?' In effect this meant, 'What shall we do to be saved?' 'Then Peter said unto them, Repent, and be baptized every one of you in the name of Jesus Christ for the remission of sins, and ye shall receive the gift of the Holy Spirit.' (Acts 2:38). Also, we know that what Jesus did had to be right. Isn't that true?"

"Oh, yes."

"Of course, Jesus did not need to be baptized. He was and is forever perfect. Nevertheless, He set the example for us by being baptized Himself. Hence, no one could ever say, 'Jesus wasn't baptized. Why should I be?' He wiped out this possible argument forever. Please look with me at Matthew 3:13-17. (Bill holds the open Bible so that Ann may look at the text and he reads all or part of it, especially verses 13 and 16.) We see that Jesus came to the Jordan River to be baptized and, after His baptism, He came up out of the water. So He definitely set the example for us, didn't He?"

"Yes, He did."

"We know also that baptism is immersion under the water. He went into and came up out of the waters of the Jordan River. Again in Romans 6 we read, 'Know ye not, that so many of us as were baptized into Jesus Christ were baptized into his death? Therefore we are buried with him by baptism into death: that like as Christ was raised up from the dead by the glory of the Father, even so we also should walk in newness of life.' (Romans 6:3,4). The words 'buried in baptism' tell us of a new birth in Christ which includes the obedience of immersion. Does that seem clear enough?"

"Yes," replies Ann, "but can this mean Spirit baptism? I've heard preachers say that baptism does not mean baptism by water."

"I have heard this argument also, but I'm sure you agree with us that the only issue here is, 'what does the Bible teach?' Is that right?"

"Of course!"

"As we just read in Matthew 3, Jesus did go to the waters of the Jordan River to be immersed, didn't He?"

"I can't deny that."

"We might also look to the tenth chapter of the book of Acts. Peter was preaching to a Gentile named Cornelius and to his household in Caesarea. The power of the Spirit was present. Peter asked, 'Can any man forbid water that these should be baptized?' (Acts 10:47). While the Holy Spirit is involved in conversion, water baptism also has a Scriptural place. In fact, the verse we referred to a while ago, Acts 2:38, tells us that we receive the Holy Spirit with baptism. How does water baptism fit into the picture? Perhaps Galatians 3:27 can make it clear: 'As many of you as have been baptized into Christ have put on Christ.' It is Christ Who saves us with His shed blood. It is Christ Who gives us the Holy Spirit. And while repentance and baptism do not save us, they bring us to Christ Who does save us. While we may not understand the full reason for water baptism, we trust the One Who said, 'He that believeth and is baptized shall be saved.' (Mark 16:16). Ought not we humans to take His word for it, Ann?"

"It would seem so."

"Now, Ann and Don, let's look at a Bible example of conversion, the one found in the last half of the eighth chapter of Acts. It begins with verse 26. Can you see on my Bible here?"

(One or more Bibles can be used in laps or on a coffee table. If it can be arranged, we like for the prospects to follow as we describe the conversion of the Ethiopian. This example of immediate obedience, and of going into and out of the water, is our reason for choosing this particular Bible conversion.)

"We can look on."

"I will not read it, but will sort of tell it in my own words while you follow along in the text, O.K.?"

"Fine!"

"Phillip had been preaching and baptizing in the region of Samaria, a central part of what we call the Holy Land. The angel of the Lord told him to go down south toward the Gaza strip. He obeyed, and encountered there a high officer of the Queen of Ethiopia who was returning home from Jerusalem in a horse-drawn chariot. He had been persuaded already that he should worship the one true God, and he had secured in Jerusalem a scroll of the Old Testament Book of Isaiah, the prophet. He was reading this while riding along the road. The Spirit moved Philip to approach him. He asked, 'Do you understand what you are reading?' 'How can I, except some man should guide me?' With this reply he invited Philip to ride along with him. The Ethiopian had been reading the prophecy that, 'He was led as a sheep to the slaughter.' Isaiah prophesied some 800 years before Christ that someone would die for us. The Ethiopian asked Philip, 'Who does the prophet refer to?' In verse thirty-five we read, 'Philip opened his mouth, and began at the same Scripture, and preached unto him Jesus.' We don't know all that Philip said to the man from Ethiopia, but we know he told him of the plan of salvation because of what follows: 'And as they went on their way, they came unto a certain water: and the eunuch said, See, here is water; what doth hinder me to be baptized? And Philip said, If thou believest with all thine heart, thou mayest. And he answered and said, I believe that Jesus Christ is the Son of God. And he commanded the chariot to stand still: and they went down both into the water, both Philip and the eunuch; and he baptized him. And when they were come up out of the water, the Spirit of the Lord caught away Philip, that the eunuch saw him no more: and he went on his way rejoicing.' (Acts 8:36-39). Here in one afternoon a man who had probably never heard of Jesus, heard about Him and His plan of salvation and became a baptized Christian -- a convert, trusting Jesus Christ completely to save him. Now, Ann, does this make sense to you?"

"Yes, it does."

"Now for the important question -- are you willing to trust the Lord Jesus Christ completely to save you?"

"Yes, I am."

"Wonderful! We praise God for your answer. We know that if we trust Him on His terms we will want to do what He says. Is that right?"

"Yes."

"He has commanded us to believe in Him, to repent and be baptized, and then to continue trusting Him. Now, Ann, will you both trust Him and obey Him?"

"Yes, I will."

(Bill extends his right hand to Ann.)

"Congratulations to you on making the most important decision of your life -- for Jesus and for heaven. Now, Ann, do you believe that Jesus is the Christ, the Son of the living God?"

"Yes, I do."

"Will you say after me, please . . . (Ann repeats after Bill each phrase.) "I believe - - that Jesus Christ - - is the Son of God - - I accept Him as my Savior - - I will trust Him for all my life."

"Ann, these are the most important words you have ever uttered. Your repentance takes place in your own heart as you turn your life over to God. The matter of immersion allows you to 'put on Christ.' The man from Ethiopia whom we just read about did not put off his baptism, did he?"

"No, he didn't."

"Ann, we keep the baptistry filled at the church. We have robes and towels ready at all times. You can in the next twenty minutes become a baptized, born again Christian. Shall we go to the church now for your baptism?"

"I hadn't thought about doing it this soon. Could I call you in a few days?"

"That is possible, but now that you have made your decision for Christ, why put off this important matter of obedience? The Bible says concerning the time to be saved, 'Now is the accepted time; behold, now is the day of salvation.' (II Corinthians 6:2). Also, we have God's warning, 'My Spirit shall not always strive with man.' (Genesis 6:3). The Holy Spirit is striving now, Ann. How about it?"

"Well . . . "

"Today can be the beginning of life eternal for you."

"All right. I am ready to go now."

"Again, we say, 'Thank God, for salvation.' Before we offer prayer and go to the church, let me come back to you for a moment, Don."

"Yes?"

"Don, you indicated that you were immersed into Christ and are satisfied with your baptism. Would you like to rededicate your life to Christ tonight, even as Ann becomes a Christian?"

"Yes, I would."

(Bill extends his hand to Don and allows Don to reconfirm his confession of faith in about the same manner as Ann made her initial confession.)

Bill says, "Shall we have prayer?" (All bow in prayer). "Thank you, Almighty God, for sending your only Begotten Son, Jesus Christ, to save us from eternal torment unto eternal life. We praise you for Ann's decision to become a Christian this very night and for Don's recommitment of life to Christ. May the Holy Spirit guide these, Thy children, daily in the experience of Christian growth. Help them to remain faithful always, living for Jesus every day of their lives. Be with us now as we go to the baptismal service to see this one whom You love, and for whom Jesus died, be buried in baptism and arise in the new life in Christ. In His matchless Name we pray. Amen."

Much more conversation must take place this same night after the baptismal service. We assume that people like Don and Ann will be members of the local congregation as of that very night unless they strongly indicate otherwise. We tell them that the important thing is their relationship to Christ, but that the church is the Bride of Christ. "Christ loved the church and gave Himself for it." (Ephesians 5:25). Follow-up will begin immediately on the basis of the general follow-up program we describe in Chapter Six.

It is very important that we line up both Don and Ann for the next service of the church. A shepherd may accompany them to the front as the invitation is being sung. They are allowed to make their confession of faith again before the congregation. The baptism is announced as having already taken place according to the Scriptural pattern of "the same hour of the night." (Acts 16:33). After the benediction the new members should be taken to the door so that all can greet them and welcome them into the fellowship.

Before this public service of introduction, the new converts have been told about the meaning of the Lord's Supper and about the fact that we follow the pattern of the early church in taking communion every Lord's Day. Hence, they will probably have taken their first communion with the local congregation even before they step to the front.

Often the new converts prefer to be baptized at a regular church service. This is always a great blessing to the entire congregation. It is important that the congregation have an opportunity to welcome the new members. If we try to do this immediately after the baptism, too many of the members will leave before the new Christians have finished dressing. Therefore, it should be a definite policy to have the newly immersed persons stand at the door with the preacher at the end of the next church service after their baptism.

## THE DECISION CARD

After the Gospel presentation, if Ann Martin had chosen to delay her baptism, a decision card would be used. In the case of a delayed baptism the card serves the double purpose of (1) helping to "nail down" the date of the planned baptism and (2) getting information for the church records. Bill Smith would assume with confidence that Ann will be baptized at the next service and would fill out a decision card, having her write her own name on it. The transfer of membership card would be used for Don. Sample cards are printed in Chapter Five. With Ann agreeing to be baptized the same hour of the night, the decision card is filled out at the church just before the baptism so that relevant information can be obtained for the church records.

## THE UNIMMERSED MEMBER OF A DENOMINATION

The example used in this chapter concerning the Don Martins gave us a look at witnessing channeled toward an immersed backslider (the husband) and a totally non-churched person (the wife). The case of Don Martin would have been handled about the same if his name had actually been on our own church membership list. The backslider is in need of this witnessing no matter where his membership is or was.

Now let us consider a person who has been in the past an active member of a denomination but who is unimmersed. In this case the presentation would go about the same, except that we would not ask, "Are you satisfied with your baptism?" We would proceed in the outline to the section on obedience and then would emphasize especially several Scripture references that teach immersion. For example:

1. Acts 2:38 where baptism is clearly commanded.
2. Matthew 3:13-17 where Jesus' baptism involved going to the Jordan River and coming up out of the water.
3. Acts 8:26-40 where the Scripture states that both Philip and the Ethiopian went down into and came out of the water.
4. Romans 6:3,4 and Colossians 2:12 which show that baptism is a burial and a resurrection.
5. John 3:23 which states that much water is needed for baptism.
6. Galatians 3:27 which teaches that baptism is for the purpose of putting on Christ.

We have found the tract by P. H. Welshimer, "Facts Concerning the New Testament Church," very helpful especially when an unimmersed person is having difficulty accepting Bible immersion. Nearly half of this tract deals with immersion.

## PUTTING OFF THE DECISION

Often when the Gospel is presented, the prospect will not make an immediate decision. Undue repetition or high pressure on our part will only drive him further away. It is important to keep loving, smiling, and winsome. We like to leave something with him such as a church brochure and a copy of our tract, "Facts Concerning Salvation," which follows the outline that we employ in witnessing.  Above all, be careful to leave an open door.  The seed has been planted and a return call may be in order in three or four weeks.  After the call is completed, be sure to fill in the prospect card with all the pertinent information about the call and date it.

On the return we let the prospect know that we know the Gospel has already been presented but we go over the material, perhaps more briefly than before, in review.  This time we spend more time actually seeking a decision and answering any excuses that he might bring up.

In presenting the Gospel, the caller needs to stay on the track but at the same time be flexible.  What we say will vary according to the prospect's needs and responses, but we try to keep to the subject and follow generally the outline.  Present the Gospel to anyone who will listen, whether he has ever been in church or not.  Stay on the general outline as long as he will let you or as long as possible without being "pushy" or rude.  Remember to leave an open door.  We never win souls by "turning people off."


## ANSWERING EXCUSES

Excuses offered by prospects make up some of the biggest problems, and hence reasons for discouragement, facing the soul-winners.  We must admit at the outset that excuses, even for the experienced caller, are difficult to cope with.  This does not necessarily mean that excuses are hard to answer with logic.  They usually are not.  But the fact that excuses are just what the word implies - - sidetracking of the real issue - - means that we are dealing more with subjective, psychological problems than with real logic.  It is better to avoid arguments by anticipating them and precluding them, but this is not always possible.  We may consider briefly the eight objections that we most often hear:

1.  "I don't feel like I'm ready yet."  This excuse is a frustrating one to the soul-winner because of its utter subjectivity.  It is hard to argue with what someone says he feels or doesn't feel. About the only way we can handle a subjective argument is to attempt to objectify it.  Try to break through the excuse by an appeal to reason.  This is necessary because the excuse is subjective but reason is objective.

We might consider with the prospect the whole structure of the plan of salvation.  Consider how it would have been if Jesus, when faced with the burden of bearing our sins on the cross, had arbitrarily said, "I'm not ready to do it yet."  Of course, He could have said this for an indefinite length of time and could still be saying to us, "I'm not ready to die for you yet."  The greatest evangelistic power centers in the message of the cross.  If we can get this message across, it can go a long way toward melting down the argument. The message of Romans 5:8, John 3:16 and I Peter 2:24 has power. These Scriptures can help us override objections in general and this one in particular. Christ is ready for us. This is what counts. One never really feels ready to break with the world. This is where Jesus comes in to help us. The Bible says, "Behold, now is the accepted time; now is the day of salvation." (II Corinthians 6:2).

2. "I'm afraid I can't live up to it." The key to answering this excuse centers in the principle of trust - - trusting Jesus completely. Marriage may be used as an illustration. God has ordained marriage for life, until severed by death. Yet the soaring divorce rate is frightening. People still enter into marriage as an accepted way of life, in spite of seeming uncertainties. A marriage maintained on love and trust will not fail.

The marriage analogy is used concerning our relationship with Christ (Matthew 22:1-14; Ephesians 5:25-32; Revelation 21:2; 22:17). Jesus showed confidence in us when He died for us; He certainly would not want to die in vain. Do we have confidence in Jesus? We are not saved by our own power, but by His power. Hence, we do not remain saved only by what we are or do, but with His help and power. Willingness to trust Him is the answer to the challenge of staying with Him faithfully after initial salvation.

In our chapter on follow-up (Chapter Six) we deal with the application of Acts 2:42. This formula for "continuing steadfastly" will definitely work. There need be no fear of falling away if we are faithful in (1) Bible study; (2) fellowship; (3) communion and (4) prayer.

We should also admit that none of us is really "living it." We are falling short of perfection. But we are "continuing steadfastly" in the faith. Salvation is not by merit but by Grace. God extends His Grace beyond conversion to our daily lives. Does this give license to sin? No; quite to the contrary, it intensifies our desire to grow in the Christian life.

3. "I don't feel the need of becoming a Christian." Again we are dealing with that ugly monster, "Mr. Subjective." Again we need to objectify before we can dialogue with any effectiveness. While salvation is often preceded by a great feeling of lostness, it can also be preceded by reason. Here we need to look at lost humanity in general, apart from any one human's feeling or lack of feeling. Going back to the Gospel outline, we are informed of man's lost condition (Romans 6:23; 3:23; Isaiah 6:5; 53:6). We fall short of God's passing grade of perfection as seen in Matthew 5:48. Hence, the Word of God can help us to feel a need that we all need to feel - - the need of salvation. If feeling isn't helping us to see our lost condition, let the Bible speak to us.

4. "There are too many hypocrites in the church." Of all the excuses encountered this one is the most "hypocritical." It is almost a case of "it takes one to know one." However, we are still dealing with a soul for whom Jesus died. People who use this excuse may actually be closer to a decision than the ones previously mentioned, because they are "grasping at straws" with their use of the old hypocrite bit. We will not be apt to convert them by saying, "There's always room for one more."

We will readily admit that there are hypocrites on the membership rolls of all churches. However, there are no hypocrites in the true church. Jesus recognized the fact that there will be pious acting hypocrites. He makes it clear that it will all be taken care of on the Judgment Day by God Himself. If we try to purge the hypocrite now, we may make the mistake of harming a sincere Christian, because our judgments are subject to error. Jesus instructs us to refrain from the attempt and to leave it to God. We read this counsel in Matthew 13:28-30.

We are all endowed with God-given freedom of choice. We will not be held responsible for another's wrong choice. Since some hypocrites choose to attend church services, I'm glad I am there with them because it is the Lord's church. He knows my heart. The hypocrite can hurt me only if I let him keep me from the Lord and from His church. Look to Jesus, and the hypocrite will fade into the background.

5. "I have difficulty in believing." This can refer to belief in God, in the Bible or both. This person has at least identified his problem. It seems to be either an intellectual problem or just another excuse. We cannot really judge the individual's sincerity. We will treat it as an intellectual problem.

To believe or not to believe? Think of the alternatives. A Frenchman (Pascal) once reflected concerning the Christian Faith, that if all the Bible claims about God, Christ, heaven, hell and salvation are false, the Christian has lost nothing by having believed it all. He has actually lived a happier life for it. On the other hand, if it is all true, the one who disbelieves has lost everything and the Christian has gained eternal life. This is really worthy of our consideration. Of course, Paul has an even better answer in, "I know in whom I have believed, and am persuaded that He is able to keep that which I have committed unto Him against that day" (II Timothy 1:12).

What is belief? It is an act of the will. We can choose to believe. Active belief is called "faith." Faith is not forced upon us. We make the choice. This is suggested by Paul as he said to a jail-keeper, "Believe on the Lord Jesus Christ and thou shalt be saved" (Acts 16:31). Start with the human will. Give faith a chance. What God has to offer is too wonderful to ignore. The question is in order, "Would you like to believe?" The fact is,

"You can believe, if you want to." The prayer of the father of the demon-possessed boy is certainly a valid one, "Lord, I believe; help thou mine unbelief" (Mark 9:24). Belief is an act of the will which, with God's help, can become assurance.

6. "There are too many churches and they all claim to be right." This is an absolutely valid observation as well as a legitimate criticism of Christendom in general. Truth is not relative; it is revealed. Truth cannot contradict truth. Agreement with the prospect's statement is in order in this case. There is something rotten in the kingdom. It would be foolish to try to justify a divided Christendom. We fully concur that it is wrong. Christ established only one church (Matthew 16:18; Ephesians 4:4,5). He prayed for its unity (John 17:21). We stand for the unity of all Christians with the Bible as the sole guide for this unity.

Admitting the error of denominationalism is one thing, but allowing this human mistake to keep us out of the Kingdom of God is quite another thing. If we look to church leaders and to denominations for absolute religious truth, we will be confused. We do not have to do this at all. Let's look to that which we can know is right. Let's look to the Bible, God's Holy Spirit inspired Word. Herein we read about the church, its beginning, its structure and the plan of salvation it is commissioned to proclaim (Matthew 16:18; Acts 2; Ephesians 4:11-13; I Corinthians 12:28; I Timothy 3; etc.). The plan of salvation is clearly revealed in the Bible (Acts 2:38; Romans 6:3,4; Galatians 3:27; etc.). We do not need to look to denominations and to the "learned clergy." Equally intelligent men contradict one another. We may look to the Word of God for final truth (see II Timothy 3:16,17).

7. "The Bible contradicts itself." This is an assertion which has been leveled against the Bible for centuries. Also this statement is made, "The Bible was written only by men."

Let's talk about the two statements together. The alleged contradictions have never been successfully produced. Every attempt to prove contradictions has failed. Upon analysis of these assertions, the more serious scholar can discover that the seeming contradiction is only a misunderstanding of the Word, or of total context and circumstances, on the part of the critic. The challenge, "Prove to me the contradiction," has never been successfully met.

Remember, the Bible is not a book of science; it is the Book of Life. However, it does not contradict true science. Where science has tried to contradict the Bible, it has itself been found wrong. Learned opinions change, but the Word of God abides forever. Its miracle of transforming broken lives rallies to its defense against all weak and flimsy criticism of God's Holy Word.

True it is that about thirty-five men wrote the Bible, but "all

Scripture is given by inspiration of God, and is profitable for doctrine, for reproof, for correction, for instruction in righteousness: that the man of God may be perfect, thoroughly furnished unto all good works" (II Timothy 3:16-17); and "For the prophecy came not in old time by the will of man: but holy men spake as they were moved by the Holy Spirit" (II Peter 1:21). The very unity of the truths revealed in the Bible, written over a period of nearly fifteen hundred years by between thirty and forty men, proves that it enjoys the Master authorship of God.

8. "The Bible is a matter of interpretation." In dealing with excuse number seven we quoted II Peter 1:21. The verse preceding it says, "Knowing this first, that no prophecy of the scripture is of any private interpretation " (II Peter 1:20).

Interpretation is in order when something is coded, cryptic or completely foreign to our usual discourse. This is not true of the Bible. Scholars have translated it from the Hebrew and Greek to the languages of the world. Comparative translations agree. Therefore the language problem is solved. We can read the Bible in the language we understand. Take God's Word as it is stated. Interpretation has no place. Read it, believe it and accept it.

Of course, the important thing to remember in answering excuses is to avoid arguments if possible. Agree whenever you can. Be positive and of good spirit in answering all excuses. Often an excuse can be anticipated and answered even before it is voiced. This is wisdom in action.

## CHAPTER FIVE

## HELPFUL MATERIALS

Certain basic materials can be helpful in the actual implementation of the soul-winners' training program. These are not "gimmick" type materials but are suggested as legitimate aids for starting and perpetuating an effective, year-round, church-wide program in personal evangelism.

The materials described in this chapter are as follows:

1. House to house survey cards
2. Prayer and Concern cards - - for securing additional prospects
3. Enlistment "Feelers" - - for seeking trainees in evangelism
4. Enlistment cards - - for signing up trainees
5. Prospect file cards
6. Decision cards
7. Workers' attendance chart
8. Report Board - - for after calling sessions
9. Religious Opinion Questionnaire
10. Workers' Diploma
11. Study materials and tracts
12. Local church brochures

It is important that we actually use and continue to use these materials after we prepare them in quantity. When such materials lie around and collect dust they become testimonies of abandoned programs. Churches in general are guilty of failing to follow through on what they start. Evangelism is one program that should never become such a casualty.

## 1. HOUSE TO HOUSE SURVEY CARD

### HOUSE TO HOUSE SURVEY

Name _____

Address _____
(Include House Number)

Member of a Church?          Yes _____          No _____

What Church and City? _____

Active?          Yes _____          No _____

Rate Prospect:   Excellent _____    Good _____    Fair _____

Name and ages of children and any other helpful information on back of card.

Name of worker _____

Date _____  19 _____
Month      Year

This is a standard 3"x5" card calling for essential but brief information. Church survey questions should be as short as possible in the interest of the time element, but card space should allow for needed information. To cover a town will mean that several hundred cards will need to be printed.

## 2. PRAYER AND CONCERN CARD

---

### PRAYER AND CONCERN CARD

I would like to see the following persons contacted and encouraged to make decisions for Christ.

Name _____ Youth or Adult _____

Address _____

Name _____ Youth or Adult _____

Address _____

Name _____ Youth or Adult _____

Address _____

☐ I will be in prayer for these persons and for the continued outreach of First Christian Church.

_____
Signed

---

The standard 3"x5" is also used here. This card is to be handed to members, inserted in bulletins or placed in pew card racks. If the use of the card is promoted properly, members can supply many names of prospects that we would not otherwise have.

## 3. ENLISTMENT "FEELERS"

The main purpose of the enlistment "feeler" is for the seeking of trainees in evangelism. This is a 5½"x8½" bulletin insert to be used during the recruitment period. This should precede the the Sunday when the actual enlistment cards are distributed. The "feeler" can help us in determining whom to seek as we try to increase our number of workers. Some will already have volunteered. Others need to be sought out.

*And he said unto them, Go ye into all the world, and preach the gospel to every creature.*
*He that believeth and is baptized shall be saved; but he that believeth not shall be damned.* Mark 16:15,16

February is recruitment month for evangelism and shepherding training. We are seeking your commitment for a four month tour of duty, March 6 to June 26. Calling is to be on Tuesday nights, or if you prefer, Wednesday mornings or Wednesday afternoons.

**Christ has called you to witness.**

Please fill out and pass to center aisle at end of service.

I am a church leader.      Yes _____      No _____

If so, please check one:    Elder ____    Deacon ____    Teacher ____

(Program is open to all Christians, church leaders and non church leaders.)

I believe in and will pray for the forthcoming evangelism training program.      Yes _____ No _____

I am interested in taking part in the program.      Yes _____ No_____

Name _____

Address _____ Phone _____

4.   ENLISTMENT CARD

**SOUL-WINNERS' TRAINING PROGRAM**

The Lord willing, I will train faithfully as a soul-winner from
_____ through _____
　　　　starting date　　　　　　　　　　　completion date

on each _____ , with goal in view of
　　　　　　　day of week

becoming a soul-winner and trainer.

_____ 　 _____
　　　　Trainee　　　　　　　　　　　Phone Number

This card can be of a standard 3"x5" size or a little larger. The dates must be put in to spell out the exact four month long tour of duty, and the calling night (or day) specified. The success of the program depends upon the team of workers being definitely committed.

## 5. PROSPECT FILE CARD
### FRONT:

Family (Last) Name _____     Husband's First Name _____

Wife's First Name _____     Youth or Single? _____

Address - Both House Number and Street — Directions if House Is Not Numbered _____

Phone Number _____     Estimated Age _____

Date Card Filled Out - Month and Year _____

Confidential Estimate _____ _____ _____ _____
                      Excellent  Good    Fair    ? ? ? ? ?

Employed Where? _____

Names and Ages of Children:     _____

_____     _____

_____     _____

Additional Helpful Information In This Space:



Visited by _____     Date and Year _____
Remarks:

Visited by _____     Date and Year _____
Remarks:

This card is 5"x8" to allow enough room for the data to be recorded and dated by the callers. This model card allows space for the record of eight visits, two on the front of the card and six on the back.

Sometimes it requires several calls to win a soul. Careful records should be kept, with dates, so that future callers will be on top of the situation in each call. We remember in a former ministry a card that stayed in our file for five years. Each call gave us a little encouragement, enough to keep us from pulling the card. The husband and wife are now very active Christians. He is a deacon and youth worker.

BACK:

| Visited by _____ | Date and Year _____ |
| Remarks: | |

| Visited by _____ | Date and Year _____ |
| Remarks: | |

| Visited by _____ | Date and Year _____ |
| Remarks: | |

| Visited by _____ | Date and Year _____ |
| Remarks: | |

| Visited by _____ | Date and Year _____ |
| Remarks: | |

| Visited by _____ | Date and Year _____ |
| Remarks: | |

## 6.  DECISION CARD

The decision cards can be of help in bringing the prospect over that final hump of commitment. Even if the decision is secured without the use of the card, it can still be employed in collecting the needed information about the convert. Another use for the card is as a tangible reminder to the prospect of the opportunity for decision. If the person seems almost but not altogether persuaded, a card may be left with him as a reminder. This can be done either just before or just after prayer is offered. It is our policy to offer prayer on all calls, whether a decision is made or not.

The decision cards are standard 3"x5" and each type of card is of a different color, one color for baptism and one for transfer.

For Baptism

```
+------------------------------------------------------------+
|                     MY  DECISION                           |
|                                                            |
|  ☐      Believing in Jesus Christ as the Son of God, I desire |
|         to commit my life to Him and His Church and to be  |
|         baptized into Christ.                              |
|                                                            |
|                 Date _____          |
|                                                            |
|  Name _____ |
|  Address _____ |
|               FIRST  CHRISTIAN  CHURCH                     |
|         Hattie Avenue       Elizabethton, Tennessee        |
+------------------------------------------------------------+
```

For Transfer

```
+------------------------------------------------------------+
|                     MY  DECISION                           |
|  ☐      Being an immersed believer in Jesus Christ, I desire to |
|         transfer my life and membership to the First Christian |
|         Church, Elizabethton, Tennessee.                   |
|                 Date _____           |
|  Notify the _____Church at       |
|  _____ |
|  Name _____ |
|  Address _____ |
|               FIRST  CHRISTIAN  CHURCH                     |
|         Hattie Avenue       Elizabethton, Tennessee        |
+------------------------------------------------------------+
```

## 7. WORKERS' ATTENDANCE CHART

| Dates | | March | | | | April | | | | May | | | | June | | | |
|---|---|---|---|---|---|---|---|---|---|---|---|---|---|---|---|---|---|
| **Names** | 6 | 13 | 20 | 27 | 3 | 10 | 17 | 24 | 1 | 6 | 15 | 22 | 29 | 5 | 12 | 19 | 26 |
| *Trainers:* | | | | | | | | | | | | | | | | | |
| Bill Mayfield | | | | | | | | | | | | | | | | | |
| Edith Hayes | | | | | | | | | | | | | | | | | |
| Etc. | | | | | | | | | | | | | | | | | |
| | | | | | | | | | | | | | | | | | |
| | | | | | | | | | | | | | | | | | |
| | | | | | | | | | | | | | | | | | |
| *Trainees:* | | | | | | | | | | | | | | | | | |
| Joe Doe | | | | | | | | | | | | | | | | | |
| Mary Smith | | | | | | | | | | | | | | | | | |
| Etc. | | | | | | | | | | | | | | | | | |
| | | | | | | | | | | | | | | | | | |
| | | | | | | | | | | | | | | | | | |
| | | | | | | | | | | | | | | | | | |
| | | | | | | | | | | | | | | | | | |

*(Chart titled: EVANGELISM AND SHEPHERDING 197-)*

## RUBBER STAMP IMAGES

     E

Star - Present        E - Excused        Red Devil - Unexcused

The attendance board should be about three feet by four feet and should be mounted on a board. Names of trainers and trainees are placed on the chart. After the names will be squares for each date of the entire four month program. An attendance secretary may be placed in charge of the stamps and stamp pads. This method of keeping roll discourages people from arbitrarily being absent.

The devil and star images may be traced from this book for the purpose of getting stamps made. A blue or black stamp pad is used for each of the stamps except the devil image. Red is used for this.

## 8. REPORT BOARD

| EVANGELISM REPORT BOARD | | | | | | | |
|---|---|---|---|---|---|---|---|
| Trainer | Date | Number of calls made | Gospel Presented? | Decisions for conversion | Decisions for transfer | Decisions for recommitment | Comments |
| | | | | | | | |
| | | | | | | | |
| | | | | | | | |
| | | | | | | | |
| | | | | | | | |
| | | | | | | | |
| | | | | | | | |
| | | | | | | | |
| | | | | | | | |
| | | | | | | | |
| | | | | | | | |
| | | | | | | | |
| | | | | | | | |
| | | | | | | | |
| | | | | | | | |
| | | | | | | | |

The report board is a large blackboard, perhaps about four feet by six feet, with permanent lines and headings painted on. The chalk spaces are below the headings. Each calling team comes back and visually plots the results after the calling session. This is excellent for post calling discussion by the teams while they are indulging in donuts and coffee.

## 9. RELIGIOUS OPINION QUESTIONNAIRE

The religious opinion questionnaire goes on a standard 8½"x11" paper. The printer can make these in pad form so that the sheets may be ripped off. Each worker may have a pad of these forms when he goes out.

# RELIGIOUS OPINION QUESTIONNAIRE

1. What is your occupation? _____
2. Are you a member of a church group? Yes____ No ____
3. Would you like to give the name of the group? _____
   Church       City
4. At what age did you become a member?
   Before 12 _____ , 12-20 _____ , 20-30 _____ , after 30 _____ .
5. At present how often do you attend?     Once a week or more_____ ,
   twice a month _____ , once a month _____ , seldom or never _____
6. Are you married?    Yes _____ No _____
7. Do you have children?     Yes _____ No _____ How many? _____
8. Are the children enrolled in Sunday School?     Yes _____ No _____
9. Who is Jesus Christ according to your understanding?     Teacher_____ ,
   Good Man _____ , Savior _____ , Other _____ .
10. In your opinion, what is God like? _____
11. How often do you read the Bible?    Daily_____ , once in a while _____ ,
    seldom or never_____ .
12. For what kind of things do you pray?    Peace _____ , Protection _____ ,
    Material things _____ , Health _____ , Spiritual things_____ ,
    Others _____ .
13. In the past year your interest in spiritual things: Increased _____ ,
    Decreased _____ , Stayed the same _____ .
14. Have you come to the place in your faith where you know for sure that you
    have eternal life? Yes _____ No _____ .
15. Do you feel the need of a more personal, saving faith? Yes _____ , No_____ .
16. Would you be willing to give us your name and address?
    Name _____
    Address _____
    Phone _____ City _____
17. Would you be willing for us to share with you how you can know for certain
    you are going to heaven? Yes _____ No _____

Thank you for your time.

Name of interviewer _____
Person interviewed was: Male _____ Female _____
Estimated age: Under 16 _____ , 16-20 _____ , 20-30_____ , Over 50
Over 50 _____ .

This type of survey is not only for gaining prospect information, but for leading into a possible witnessing opportunity. This opportunity may come while interviewing the person. This is not to be confused with the area survey we described earlier. The opinion survey can develop into immediate witnessing.

If the time should come that the prospect file is almost dry, teams may be assigned streets to work. They may go from house to house, and still in teams of three. It is desirable to gain entry into the home while asking the opinions on the form. Often people enjoy being encountered for opinion surveys. This is not a gimmick but a method of seeking open doors for witnessing. People can be encountered without prior knowledge of their names.

I'm quite sure that the Jesuralem church had no prospect file; they covered the city and country-side witnessing (Acts 8:4). The file is a great aid in directing us to those whom we believe to be the more prospective of the prospects. However, it would be a terrible mistake to stop witnessing because we think we have run out of good prospects. People are all about us, probably more than fifty per cent of whom are lost; hence, we should not refuse to witness simply because we do not know who these people are. The cults use the door to door method with some effectiveness. There is no reason why the carriers of God's Truth cannot go door to door. The opinion questionnaire is an aid to this kind of evangelism.

The opinion questionnaire may be used by the teams, and by Christian youth groups, in the shopping centers and on the streets. If we feel that we need some city or shopping center authorization for this kind of work, the proper people may be contacted. Hopefully, permission would be granted. One church launched a city wide campaign with the opinion questionnaire and had the questions published in the local paper. After this they hit the shopping centers with some results.

The approach at homes or on the streets will be very similar to that made in the process of a regular call. We introduce ourselves, identify our church and then we relate to the person that we are taking a religious opinion survey. We ask for some of the person's time and proceed with the questions. As we approach the latter part of the questionnaire, we come to subject matter definitely geared to the Gospel. If the person seems willing, especially if it is in his home, we can present the Gospel outline and seek a decision. Or an appointment may be made for a future encounter. If no definite appointment is made, but the person seems receptive, a drop in call would be in order in the near future.

With the religious opinion questionnaire on hand, calling never needs to slow down for want of known prospects.

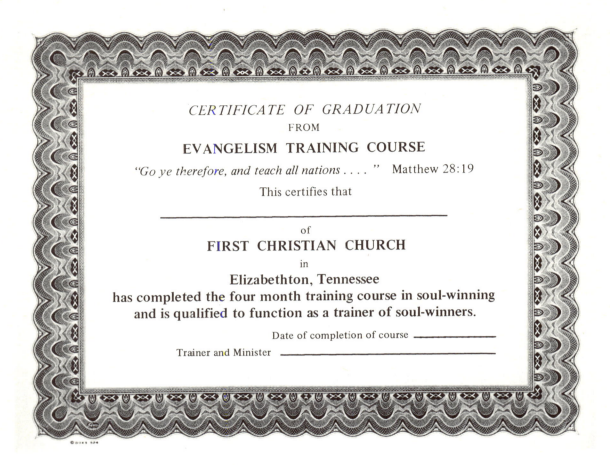

*CERTIFICATE OF GRADUATION*

FROM

**EVANGELISM TRAINING COURSE**

*"Go ye therefore, and teach all nations . . . . "*   Matthew 28:19

This certifies that

_____

of

**FIRST CHRISTIAN CHURCH**

in

**Elizabethton, Tennessee**
**has completed the four month training course in soul-winning**
**and is qualified to function as a trainer of soul-winners.**

Date of completion of course _____

Trainer and Minister _____

8½"x11" diploma in green color  (GOES 912)

The diploma blank is copyrighted by the Goes Lithographing Company of Chicago (42 West 61st Street, zip code 60621). It is printed here by permission and is not to be reproduced. Printers have this stock on hand or can order it from the Goes Company. You choose the wording to be printed on the Goes form. Your local printer will do the word printing in his own shop.

The diplomas may be presented to the graduates in evangelism at a regular church service.

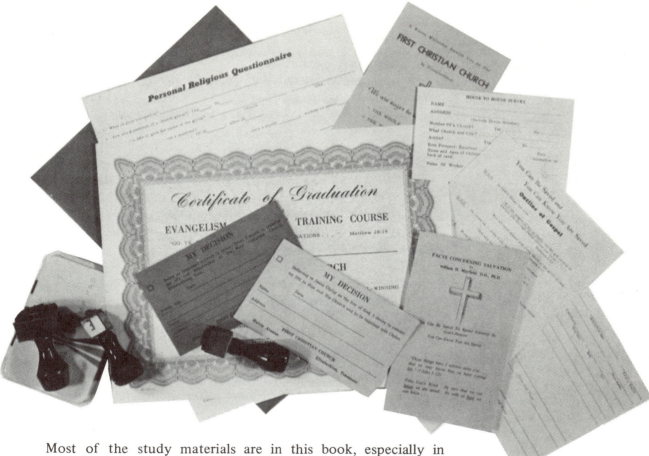

Most of the study materials are in this book, especially in Chapters Three and Four. The Gospel outline, in the shorter and longer forms, and the outline with Scriptures are for drilling and memorization. The Gospel tract, printed in Chapter Four, is an aid to study as well as an actual tract. Outline memorization and Scripture memorization must come before a person can make the presentation a part of himself.

Of course, we would like to suggest that this book be placed in the hands of all trainees. This suggestion has merit only if it is agreed that possession of the book will definitely help the trainee to learn to present the Gospel effectively. The learning outlines are included in Chapter Four for this express purpose.

The tract, "Facts Concerning Salvation," is geared to the outline. These tracts are obtainable in quantity. Primarily the tract is for the purpose of being presented to all prospects. But it is also a study guide for the trainee in evangelism. Memorization may begin with a shorter outline like the one that follows and then proceed to the memorizing of the fuller outlines and Gospel presentation itself.

*YOU CAN BE SAVED and*
*YOU CAN KNOW YOU ARE SAVED*

## OUTLINE OF GOSPEL

**<u>Man</u> - In God's Image but lost.**
*For the wages of sin is death; but the gift of God is eternal life through Jesus Christ our Lord.*      Romans 6:23
*For all have sinned and come short of the glory of God.*      Romans 3:23

**<u>God</u> - He loves us - John 3:16, but Sin must be punished.**
*God will by no means clear the guilty.*      Exodus 34:7

**<u>Grace</u> - Free Gift of Salvation which we cannot earn.**
*But we believe that through the grace of the Lord Jesus Christ we shall be saved.*      Acts 15:11

**<u>Jesus</u> - He brings God's Grace to us.**
*The blood of Jesus Christ cleanseth us from all sin.*      I John 1:7
*Who His own self bare our sins in His own body on the tree . . . by whose stripes we are healed.*      I Peter 2:24

**<u>Faith</u> - More than head belief - Faith is trust in Christ for salvation.**
*Thou believest that there is one God; thou doest well: the devils also believed, and trembled.*      James 2:19
*Faith is the substance of things hoped for, and the evidence of things not seen.*      Hebrews 11:1

**<u>Obedience</u> - Salvation is a free gift from God which we can receive by faith and obedience.**
*He that believeth and is baptized shall be saved; and he that believeth not shall be damned.*      Mark 16:16

**<u>Assurance</u> - You can Know you are saved.**
*These things have I written unto you . . . that ye may know that ye have eternal life.*      I John 5:13

## 12.   LOCAL CHURCH BROCHURES

A sample church brochure follows for your consideration. Many variations can be worked out to fit a local church program.

**A Warm Welcome Awaits You
At The**

**FIRST CHRISTIAN CHURCH**
In Elizabethton

*We are eager to serve*

  † THE WHOLE FAMILY

  † THE WHOLE COMMUNITY

    † WORSHIP

    † WITNESS

    † STUDY

    † FELLOWSHIP

    † CHRISTIAN OUTREACH

513 Hattie Avenue
(Downtown Elizabethton)

| 542-5651 | 543-1422 | 543-3414 |
| Office | Study | Parsonage |

*The end of your search
    for a friendly church*

———————————

Front Side

**The First Christian Church**
of Elizabethton, Tennessee

*Preaching Christ Crucified,
    Risen and Coming Again*

It is our desire to be Christ centered, Bible believing, evangelistic. It is our purpose to restore the Church of the Bible.

Nearly two thousand years ago Jesus Christ founded one church. We strive to recapture the spirit of the first century church by accepting the Bible as our only guide. We claim no creed but Christ and wear no name but "Christian." We are a part of no denominational structure. We are of the body of Christ only.

———————————

Back Side

**DR. WILLIAM H. MAYFIELD**
*Minister*

### COME WORSHIP WITH US
**Each Lord's Day:**

| | |
|---|---|
| Worship | 10:00 A.M. |
| Bible School for all ages | 11:00 A.M. |
| Youth Hour | 6:30 P.M. |
| Evening Evangelistic Hour | 7:30 P.M. |

**Each Wednesday:**

| | |
|---|---|
| Prayer Meeting | 7:30 P.M. |

*NURSERY PROVIDED*

WE BELIEVE —

In Jesus Christ the only begotten Son of God
(Matthew 16:16).

In the absolute Divine Inspiration of the Bible
(II Timothy 3:16,17).

In restoring the spirit, doctrine and power of the first century church
(Acts 2:42).

In evangelism as the first business of the church
(Mark 16:15,16).

In full obedience to all of the Bible plan of salvation
(Mark 16:16; Acts 2:38; Romans 6:3,4).

Inside

This particular brochure is 7½"x8" before it is folded; hence, 3¾"x8" folded. This is an ideal brochure size. It can be left with prospects, and left in the door when the prospect is not at home.

The tract, "Facts Concerning Salvation," is an aid to witnessing. It provides a printed outline of the Gospel to coincide with what was presented verbally. The prospect can read it with greater understanding after having heard a Christian present the Gospel.

The brochure helps to tie the truth of the Gospel into a local church and its program. Hence, both tract and brochure should be left with prospects. Every possible aid leading toward a decision for Christ should be employed.

## CHAPTER SIX

## FOLLOWING UP CONVERSIONS

Statistics are frightening. The number of Americans killed on the highways each year, the number who die of heart disease and cancer, the crime rate per capita, juvenile crime, the soaring divorce rate, the number of young people who have experimented with narcotics - - staggering statistics indeed are all of these. However, the professional statisticians do not generally deal with the most serious statistics of all - - the number of one-time members of the Body of Christ who have fallen away, who are now on the pathway to eternal hell.

Evangelism is serious business, but follow-up is equally serious. What good have we done in winning a person, hearing him confess Christ and seeing him baptized, if he falls away and dies lost, doomed to the same hell that was his destination before he was evangelized? Our Lord's commission to us is (1) to baptize and (2) to teach them to observe all things after baptism (Matthew 28:19-20).

## FOLLOW-UP GOALS

Our purpose in the follow-up program is to help the new Christian to arrive at the spiritual growth level which will maximize his chances of remaining forever a saved person. Accomplishing this, along with initial evangelism, is the full-time job of the church. It involves teaching, counselling and fellowshipping. It involves the energetic action of Christian love.

The new Christian has not had sufficient follow-up until (1) he can say with confidence that he is sure of his salvation and (2) he is completely involved in the fellowship and program of the local church. This latter goal is realized when, and only when, the convert has accepted the people of the local congregation as his people and when his social life, as well as religious life, centers in the church. Also, he is involved to the point that he will find or form this kind of Christian fellowship if he moves elsewhere. Anything short of this is not likely to endure.

While it is true that some converts will drift away, some even before getting off to a good start, the losses can be at least minimized by effective follow-up. With poor follow-up by the church, losses in an average community of today may run forty-five per cent of all additions. Effective follow-up can very conceivably bring these losses to as low as twenty per cent. This gain in conservation of twenty-five permanently saved souls out of every hundred is certainly worth all of the effort. In other words, we may keep fifty-five out of one-hundred additions with a poor program, but a good program should enable us to keep eighty out of one hundred. Our follow-up activity should be such that we know we have made every reasonable effort to conserve every evangelized soul.

## FOLLOW-UP AND CHURCH GROWTH

The growth of a local congregation actually depends more upon good follow-up than on initial evangelism. Some congregations report large numbers of additions but are unable to report noticable increases in church attendance. Other congregations reporting much fewer additions seem to grow steadily in attendance. Why this seeming contradiction?

Part of the answer may be in the nature of the church field. A city may be growing but at the same time have a high population turn-over rate. In this field a church may need one-hundred additions a year just to hold its own in attendance. And it will not even hold its own if its follow-up program is not effective. Regardless of the nature of the population center (growing with high turn-over, growing with low turn-over, or not growing but stable), all fields are white unto the harvest. Any population center will have lost people who can be found and witnessed to. Therefore, the key to growth lies in both evangelism and follow-up. The possibility is strong that the growing church is the church with a good follow-up program. In the church growth picture, follow-up makes the difference.

## IMPLEMENTING FOLLOW-UP

Evangelism aims toward the goal of bringing a lost person to an obedient faith in Christ. The convert's baptism is a dramatic climax to this activity. Follow-up, however, is a long continuing labor of love which is aimed at teaching the new Christian to observe all things as commanded in the Word. The size and complexity of this job calls for a working team of church leaders. It will not succeed if it is left up to a one man preacher taskforce. The preacher will need to organize the follow-up program and put it into action, but he will need to have his church leadership active in it on a permanent basis. Even as personal evangelists have to be trained, the working shepherds also have to be trained to do their job in the follow-up.

All of the church elders plus as many deacons as can be secured should be recruited for tours of duty in the two-fold work of (1) following up on new members and (2) shepherding older members who are drifting away. Others, including women and youth, should also be sought to help in this work under the direction of the minister and chairman of the elders. These people may or may not double in the evangelism training program. However, it should not be necessary to rob from the evangelism personnel in favor of the follow-up program. Active Christians not involved in evangelism can be encouraged to rise and shine in shepherding and follow-up.

The shepherding/follow-up workers may be signed up for the same definite tour of duty as the workers in evangelism and for the same time periods. However, care must be taken to prevent the double program from becoming too cumbersome. This danger may be overcome with careful planning. An excellent plan is to have all of the recruited shepherds meet from 6:00 to 7:00 each Sunday evening during the four month tour of duty. Teaching and planning takes place, and contact assignments are made at this time. This same group should assemble again on Tuesday, or some other designated night, to make the actual contacts with new or drifting Christians. A definite night is needed to avoid procrastination on the part of the shepherding callers.

The follow-up workers will need to be led by someone other than the preacher since he will be tied up with the evangelism. He can, however, do at least part of the teaching. These workers can assemble in a different room from the evangelism workers and can work from an entirely different file. It is important to avoid confusing the two programs one with the other and hence weakening both. Even as the personal evangelists are trained to do their job in soul-winning effectively, the shepherds are trained to teach and lead the new Christians into life-long faithfulness. Usually the workers in evangelism fully realize that the actual work of evangelizing is not complete until the converts are established as faithful members of the Body of Christ. Hence, some of these workers desire to be in both programs in order to be involved in the full action. This is highly desirable when the worker's time allows his participation in both programs. If the calling for both groups is on the same night, the worker who is doubling his effort to be included in both programs will have to make his shepherding calls on another night. He will then make his report at the 6:00 P.M. Sunday meeting of the shepherds.

The church elders may be employed as the trainers for the follow-up callers. The teaming up may be fairly flexible. The first three calls on the new convert may be made by the minister, the minister of education and a follow-up team, in that order. After this, a call should be made by some member of a Sunday School class of the convert's age group and then by a representative of the ladies' circle or the men's fellowship. The follow-up team will need to enlist specific people to make the calls. Each call may include a team of from one to three in number.

Why all of this? Man is not only a religious creature but he is also a social creature. If the new Christian is involved only in worship and not in the social stream of the church, he is not likely to endure. The reverse of this, as seen for example in the person who attends only Sunday School, is equally a spiritual disaster.

## SCHEDULE OF CONTACTS AND USE OF MATERIALS

Let's do all that we can to involve totally the new Christian in the affairs of Christ and His church. Such involvement is the key to the convert's spiritual development. An active church life and a healthy devotional life usually go hand in hand. About two contacts a week can be made during the month following the conversion. Delay in making these contacts may mean the casualty of the soul. Even as a new babe needs constant care, the new Christian needs spiritual care immediately after conversion. We suggest the following schedule:

1. The preacher makes a visit by the second day after the conversion.
2. The director of Christian Education calls two days later.
3. A call is made by the shepherds early in the second week (eighth or ninth day after conversion).
4. A caller from a Sunday School class appears near the end of the second week after the conversion. This is the fourth contact in fourteen days.
5. During the third week a person from the ladies' organization, men's fellowship or youth group makes a call - - depending on age, interest and sex of the convert.
6. During the fourth week after the conversion either the preacher or a shepherd should contact the new Christian to attempt to involve him or her in some definite church responsibility.
7. A month before a new soul-winner's training program begins, the new Christian may be sought for recruitment in the program of evangelism.

At this point it will be well for us to consider in more detail the above suggested visits and the materials that may be used to enhance Christian growth on the part of the new Christian.

1. <u>The preacher makes a visit by the second day after the conversion</u>. He congratulates the person again for his important life decision and elaborates from the Bible the responsibilities and privileges of the Christian life. He may present at this time a packet which includes (1) a baptismal and/or membership certificate; (2) a Bible (these may be secured in quantity, hard-

backed and very reasonably priced, from the American Bible Society); (3) a church brochure with times of all services; (4) a church directory; (5) a new converts' study book (<u>Studies for New Converts</u> by Price Roberts is a good one to use); (6) a new member's brochure; (7) a covenant book (see below for a sample); and any other additional helpful material.

A new member's brochure can be composed by the minister. The exact nature of the brochure may vary from church to church, depending upon the local program. The first pages can include letters from the minister(s), church board, ladies' groups, Sunday School, etc. A short doctrinal statement can explain the what and why of the Christian church. Some advice for Christian growth based on Acts 2:42 and other passages can be included. An orientation section in the brochure can acquaint the convert with all local church services and opportunities. In addition to worship services and Bible study opportunities, most churches have ladies' and men's fellowship and service groups, youth activities, scouts, nursery services, etc. The new member's brochure should be complete with all of this information. Christian service opportunities should be listed, because the new Christian is urged to become totally involved in the work of the church. He is also invited to call upon the minister and elders at any time for help and counselling. The brochure would not be complete without a section on stewardship. Tithing, for example, is a means of great personal blessing for the Christian (Malachi 3:8-10). Stewardship is very much a part of our spiritual growth.

A sample covenant book is reproduced here for your consideration. The book is about 3½" by 5" folded.

## THE CHURCH WELCOMES YOU

To become a part of the body of Christ, a person must Believe on Him – Repent of his sins – Confess His name before men – and be buried with Him in the waters of baptism.

Baptism alone will not save a person – nor will Repentance alone – nor will Faith alone. It is the baptism of the penitent believer in Christ that brings salvation or remission of sins. Besides it brings the promise of eternal life and the gift of the Holy Spirit.

One who has become a citizen in the Kingdom of God must be loyal to the King. Regularity in attending the services of the Church should be the plan, purpose and platform of every citizen.

The early Christians "continued steadfastly in the Apostles doctrine, fellowship, breaking of bread and prayer." The Christian today must be no less steadfast in these basic elements of the Faith.

You have a church home and a pastor. These are valuable assets and become more precious with the years. Avail yourself of the services of both in any time of crisis.

*PAGE 1*

---

*This is to Certify that*

_____

*was received by*

_____

*into the membership of the*

*FIRST CHRISTIAN CHURCH*

*of Elizabethton, Tennessee*

*on*

_____

_____
Pastor

*PAGE 2*

---

## MY COVENANT WITH GOD AND THE CHURCH

Now that I have identified myself with the Church I gladly accept the responsibility which God imposes on membership. My responsibity is measured by my talents, education, ability and material resources.

1. I shall strive to be faithful in attendance for the regular services of the church. (Hebrews 10:25)
2. I shall endeavor to render some form of Christian service.
3. As the Lord prospers me, I shall give regularly to the support of His Church.
4. I shall pray regularly, not only for myself, but for the work of the church – especially that souls may be brought into the Kingdom of God.

_____
*Signed*

_____
*Date*

*PAGE 3*

---

## YOUR FINANCIAL OBLIGATION TO THE CHURCH

Each new member has a sincere desire to bear his share of the cost of maintaining the church. Our work is maintained by voluntary contributions. We do not "assess" any member but depend on the regular, systematic giving of each Christian.

How much should a new member give? Let your conscience and God's Word be your guide. The principle of the tithe was operative in Patriarchal and Mosaic dispensations. The Lord Jesus and His Apostles endorsed it. (Read Malachi 3:8-10; Matthew 23:23; I Corinthians 9:14). We strongly urge all our members to practice this. Remember that if circumstances and necessity prevent you from giving you are most welcome in the church just the same.

*PAGE 4*

There is a possibility of combining the covenant book and the brochure if so desired.

2. <u>Director of Christian Education calls within four days of the conversion</u>. He also welcomes the new Christian and acquaints him with the total Christian Education program of the church. He may have a prepared mimeo-sheet listing all Sunday School and special classes available. The Sunday evening program of training fellowship should be promoted, along with the evening service that follows it. The Wednesday night program and all Bible study and prayer gatherings should be recommended. The youth work for all ages of children and young people is also presented. A packet of sample literature and publications may be given to the new member for his or her consideration.

This would be an excellent time for the "Interest and Talent Survey" form. A sample follows. The convert may fill out the form while the caller waits or it can be secured later the same day . . .

# INTEREST AND TALENT SURVEY
# FIRST CHRISTIAN CHURCH

Name _____ Phone _____

Address _____

Occupation _____ Date _____

Age ☐ Under 25 ☐ 25-30 ☐ 30-40 ☐ 40-50 ☐ 50-60 ☐ Over 60

Please indicate by a check (√) mark your talent or interest in the following areas of activity. If not interested in an area, please leave it blank.

## CHURCH ADMINISTRATION
Leadership training will be arranged for those desiring to serve.
____ 1. Elder
____ 2. Deacon
____ 3. Committee Member (indicate 1st and 2nd choice)
____ 4. Christian Education
____ 5. Worship
____ 6. Ushering
____ 7. Recreation
____ 8. Personal Work
____ 9. Missionary
____ 10. Finance
____ 11. Welfare
____ 12. Property

## CHRISTIAN EDUCATION
Leadership training will be arranged for those desiring to serve.
____ 13. Teacher (Age ____)
____ 14. Class Officer
____ 15. Superintendent or Dept. Supt.
____ 16. Youth Sponsor (Age ____)
____ 17. Vacation Bible School (Age ____)
____ 18. Scout Leader
____ 19. Athletic Coach (Sport _____)
____ 20. Records (Secretary)
____ 21. Librarian
____ 22. Projectionist or Film Librarian

## MUSIC
____ 23. Piano
____ 24. Organ
____ 25. Solo
____ 26. Group Singing
____ 27. Choir Member
____ 28. Instrumentalist, Instrument Played
_____

## PUBLIC RELATIONS
____ 29. Visitation
____ 30. Cradle Roll
____ 31. Call on new people in town
____ 32. Call on resident visitors to our services
____ 33. Call on hospital sick and shut-ins
____ 34. Call on inactive members
____ 35. Call on bereaved
____ 36. Call on new members
____ 37. Call on very interested prospective members (Evangelism)
____ 38. Telephone
____ 39. Correspondence (Cards, Letters)
____ 40. Newspaper, Radio, TV
____ 41. Ushering
____ 42. Photography
____ 43. Hospitality to overnight guests
____ 44. Provide transportation
____ 45. Campaign leader

## PERSONAL SKILLS
____ 46. Art Work - Posters, etc.
____ 47. Typing
____ 48. Office Work
____ (Filing, etc.)
____ 49. Cooking
____ 50. Carpentering
____ 51. Painting
____ 52. Landscaping
____ 53. Floral Arranging
____ 54. Electrical Work
____ 55. Nursery Work (Child Care)
____ 56. Public Address System

## DRAMATICS
____ 57. Director or Coach
____ 58. Participant in Drama
____ 59. Costumes, Props, Lighting

3. <u>A call is made by the shepherds about the eighth day after conversion</u>.

The shepherding/follow-up teams of callers are directed by the elders and together they make up the teaching and cultivation task force. These are the people who are working to implement a well organized follow-up program. It is important for them to be prepared for a personal teaching job even as the personal evangelists are prepared for the initial presentation of the Gospel.

A good variety of tracts and study materials should be made available to these teams. Among these would be studies on the Lord's Supper, stewardship, worship and related subjects. Our publishing houses have good supplies and varieties of this kind of material to choose from. The shepherds will also present the offering envelopes and explain the stewardship structure of the Lord's Church, unless they delegate this to a capable member of the finance committee. The Biblical tithe should be emphasized (see Leviticus 27:30; Malachi 3:8-10; Matthew 23:23; Matthew 5:20, Hebrews 7:8, etc.).

The follow-up chairman and his workers will have the responsibility of scheduling the remaining contacts as outlined above. After all of these contacts have been made it will be the job of the follow-up crew to keep tab on the new Christians as well as on older ones who are in danger of drifting. This work must be kept alive to minimize backsliding.

The teaching element of the follow-up should be firmly founded in the Scriptures. Among passages for use are: Acts 2:42; Revelation 2:10; II Peter 3:18; Romans 12:1,2; Matthew 26:26-30; Philippians 4:8; I Peter 2:5; II Peter 1:5-9; and Hebrews 6:1-6. (When using the Hebrews 6 passage it is important to note that the word 'seeing' in verse 6, K.J.V., is continuing action in the Greek language and means 'while we continue to crucify the Son of God afresh.' Hence, there is hope for the backslider through total repentance.)

We recommend the following "Now That You Are Saved" study guide to help in teaching the new Christians:

# NOW THAT YOU ARE SAVED
### You Can Be Saved and You Can <u>Know</u> You Are Saved (I John 5:13)
### AND
### You Can Be Absolutely Sure of Staying Saved Forever
### IF . . .
### If and Only If You Follow God's Plan for Christian Growth
### † † † † † † †

God has revealed His plan of salvation and God has revealed His plan for staying saved forever.

**ASSURANCE FOR ETERNITY** — Revelation 2:10 commands us to be faithful unto death to be eternally saved. How do we remain faithful unto death? In Acts 2:42 we have a one verse formula for staying saved forever. It says, "*And they continued steadfastly in the APOSTLES' DOCTRINE, and FELLOWSHIP, and in BREAKING OF BREAD, and in PRAYERS.*" (Acts 2:42). If you do these things after baptism, you will never fall from God's saving grace.

Continue faithfully in:

1. **APOSTLES' DOCTRINE** — A Christian should study the Bible, both the New Testament and the Old Testament every day. Be sure your daily Bible reading includes the New Testament. (II Timothy 2:15).   *Bible Reading*

   To fail to read the New Testament for even one day is to make one step toward backsliding. If you use two book markers you can read both the New Testament and Old Testament every day.

2. **FELLOWSHIP** — Worship with the people of God regularly. Hebrews 10:25 says not to neglect it. Even one worship service missed is a step toward backsliding.   *Worship*

   It is very important for Christian growth to be in <u>both</u> the worship services and in a Sunday School class. The class offers both Bible study and the fellowship of a smaller group. A Christian will not stay a Christian for very long unless he has this kind of fellowship with other Christians.

3. **BREAKING OF BREAD** — Weekly observance of the communion is necessary. John 6:53 teaches us that we are spiritually dead without it. Acts 20:7 infers that the early church communed weekly.   *Communion*

   Taking communion every week keeps our baptism alive. In baptism we relate to the death and resurrection of Jesus (Romans 6:4). In the communion we do this weekly. Herein lies continuing spiritual strength.

4. **PRAYER** — A Christian should begin and end the day with prayer, and should pray often every day. (I Thessalonians 5:17).   *Prayer*

   These four things will keep you saved forever, and will keep you growing as a Christian. Your growth should lead you into witnessing to others about Christ.

**Follow the four-fold program of Acts 2:42 and you will stay saved forever.**

*"These things have I written unto you . . . that ye may know that ye have eternal life."* (I John 5:13)

This form can be printed in quantity to present to all new Christians. It may be copied as it is or it may be modified. We feel that the Acts 2:42 approach is vital. If a Christian (1) studies his Bible daily, both the New Testament and Old, as the continuing steadfastly in the "Apostles' doctrine" implies, (2) fellowships with the church regularly, (3) communes weekly as the "breaking of bread" implies and (4) prays daily, he will not backslide. For this reason Acts 2:42 is a tremendously important follow-up Scripture.

Also the "Now that I am a Christian" home film strip series may be purchased and used by the elders and shepherds. A program for this should be set up with all new Christians. Our Christian book stores and publishing houses have full information on this kind of valuable material.

The follow-up shepherds are responsible for the continuing cultivation of new Christians until they are truly working as followers of our Lord and are totally involved in His church.

4. <u>A visitor from a Sunday School class, or from more than one class, appears during the second week after conversion.</u>

This visit is arranged by the follow-up leaders who keep a close liaison between new Christians and the Sunday School department. The shepherds must make certain that this contact is made. Since man is a social creature as well as religious, it is imperative that we direct the new Christian to the smaller fellowship group of a Bible School class. Here is where people get to know people and where Christians mix socially as well as assemble for Bible study.

Weekly meetings of the shepherds are vitally needed to plan out and implement these contacts of Sunday School classes and leaders with converts, as well as for overall planning. A casual assignment will not guarantee that the job will be accomplished. The leaders of the follow-up program must not only follow up conversions but must also follow up on the workers assigned to help in the program. We should allow the Sunday School department no peace until its part in follow-up is accepted and fulfilled. If the new convert is attending worship services, but is not involved in smaller fellowship groups within the church, he will probably feel like an outsider. Hence his chances for spiritual survival will be greatly decreased.

5. <u>During the third week after conversion a person from the ladies' organization, men's fellowship or youth groups makes a visit.</u> As is true for each visit, the number of callers may be from one to three.

The age and sex of the convert, along with family status and areas of interest, will lead the shepherds of the follow-up program to hand pick the persons to make this particular contact. The purpose here is to get the new Christians completely involved. If we leave it up to the convert to take the initiative to include himself or herself in the special church affairs, the involvement will probably not occur. Hence the door is left widely open for backsliding.

We must teach our people to go out of their way to include the new person in all fellowship aspects of the church. This means the sincere and open offering of ourselves in personal friendship. The church with its little cliques and closed fellowship groups will not succeed in evangelism. Open all possible doors for this newly claimed soul. The social levels of the world must be equalized in the church of our Lord who gave ninety per cent of His time and energy to the poor. The wife of the $40,000 a year executive will have a warm and comfortable fellowship with her circle member who is on welfare, if the church is truly Christian.

6. <u>By the fourth week after the conversion either the preacher or a shepherd should contact the new Christian, or new transferee, to involve him or her in some definite church responsibility.</u>

The talent and interest survey sheet should already have been studied. Now the shepherd will converse with the new member about a definite service he can render for His Lord. We go on the firm assumption that the new member is willing to be of service. It is in this area that spiritual conservation truly wins out. When a Christian is willing to serve the Lord, he is not likely to backslide. Hence this particular contact is of utmost importance.

For its own use the follow-up team should have a mimeographed list of all possible areas of service within the structure of the local church. They should be aware of where the greatest needs are for recruiting workers. Talent sheets are studied and then personal contacts made. However, this should be done after the approval of the minister and/or elders. It would be tragic to line up a new Christian for a job and then have to tell him that he can't be used in this area at this time.

Teaching assignments and work on certain committees will probably need clearance. The area of service is wide. Participation is possible in the choir, nursery, transportation committee, youth committee and in scores of other service areas. Conversion and follow-up is not complete until the newly gained soul is involved in Christian service. It is in this area that so many churches fail in the conservation of souls.

7. <u>The involvement of a new Christian in evangelism.</u> This is nearly always desirable. We have seen spiritual giants develop in the matter of weeks because of their commitment to evangelism.

Therefore, during the recruitment months leading into a round of evangelism training, the new converts and other additions that have been added during the past year should be definitely approached. Often the newer Christians make some of the better personal evangelists. Years of "churchanity" has not chilled their enthusiasm for the Lord.

## ADDITIONS BY TRANSFER

The same general follow-up plan is used for the Christian who comes by transfer. This program can be varied to fit the need of each transferee. For example, an active church family may move to town and take fellowship almost immediately. The above plan of teaching may be ninety percent deleted in this case. The rest of the plan would be followed, however.

On the other hand, more than fifty percent of transfers in the average church may also be coming by rededication. In these cases the complete follow-up with teaching should ensue.

We should not assume that an immersed person coming for the hand of fellowship is a mature Christian. He may or may not be. He may be an immersed backslider. If rededication is in order, this can be done by the transferee even as he receives fellowship. Hence two happenings are occurring - - reconsecration of life and transfer of membership. Make this clear to the person and to the congregation. Then gear the follow-up to the individual's need.

## KEEPING THE FOLLOW-UP ALIVE

The follow-up/shepherding team is made up of recruits for this phase of the evangelism program. They should be active in this work during the four month tour of duty and throughout the year. Two four month tours will take care of eight months out of the year, but the other four months should not be entirely neglected. Follow-up is the work of "teaching them to observe all things" (Matthew 28:20). This will require a continuing and permanent program. We should never allow evangelism and follow-up to be pushed to the sidelines. The team is dealing with two challenges: (1) nurturing the new members and (2) salvaging the older members who are in the process of drifting away.

The membership file and the list of new members taken from the file must be ever before us in the implementation of a lasting follow-up program. We should not let even one soul slip away without making every prayerful effort to help the person stay in a saved state. We should never consider the follow-up job completed.

Our goal is many-fold, but three special goals should be before us continually:

1. The Christian is totally involved in the over-all church fellowship and in smaller group fellowships such as Bible School classes, ladies' circles, men's fellowship, youth groups, etc.

2. The Christian has a place of service in the church.

3. The Christian is certain of his salvation. "These things have I written unto you . . . that ye may know you have eternal life" (I John 5:13).

*CHAPTER SEVEN*

## EVALUATIONS AND REFLECTIONS

It is most evident that a program in evangelism such as described in these pages will be very expensive in the precious commodities of time and energy. This is certainly true of the program employed by Dr. James Kennedy in his "Evangelism Explosion" as well as the programs, for example, of our own George Stansberry and Reggie Thomas. This is true of the work of evangelism which took place in Asia Minor during the First Century A.D. when 3000 and 5000 and multitudes were added to the Lord (Acts 2:41; 4:4; 5:14 and 6:7). Without this expenditure of dedicated time and energy the church today cannot even begin to obey the Great Commission of our Lord.

Is it worth the effort? How much is a soul worth? Should a church revolutionize its traditional program(s) to bring year-round evangelism to the front every year? Indeed, the true restoration of New Testament Christianity will give spiritual birth to congregations of people who are completely sold on and involved in evangelism. The realization of this goal, however, must be triggered by prayerful resolution as well as actual commitment to the program.

## WHAT EVANGELISM DOES FOR A FIELD

The average field of labor, or general church community, is more unevangelized than evangelized. This is especially true since the stable community almost everywhere is giving place to the transient. Even if a field was well evangelized last year, it needs the same Gospel impact this year. The population turn-over will keep almost any field ripe unto harvest.

We live in a day in which the social type Bible prophecies are being fulfilled before our eyes. Jesus prophesied the reoccurrence of the society of "the days of Noah" (Matthew 24:37). Peter tells of the last days and the "scoffers, walking after their own lust" (II Peter 3:3). Paul prophecies that "the time will come when they will not endure sound doctrine" (II Timothy 4:3). Behold, this is our field of evangelism in what seems to be the last generations of the latter days. While the field is sinful by nature, even in the now fading Bible belt, the Gospel still makes a difference. Every soul won to Jesus betters the community and adds at least some balm in Gilead. From a pure social standpoint evangelism is a must. It is the only hope for basic social survival and it is the single hope of eternal life through Jesus Christ.

# WHAT EVANGELISM DOES FOR A CHURCH

The traditional church has been an object of much controversy for almost a generation now. Is the church as we knew it in the 1940's and 1950's still relevant today? Is it accomplishing its mission of helping people in the here and now and saving people for the hereafter?

There was a day when fair numbers of lost people would come to church and would visit revivals. Souls have been won by pulpit exhortation. Mass evangelism on a small scale enjoyed some success in yesteryears. Now such evangelism requires the presence of a religious celebrity in a big city arena amidst an atmosphere and glitter of a Park Avenue public relations program. This kind of endeavor reaches some of the big cities but usually has little effect upon the more remote fields.

Today in the average church service few prospects are in attendance. Never, since the first century A.D., has personal evangelism been more vital than now. Church must be carried to the non-attending sinner if he is to be won to the Lord. The church can no longer survive as a worship retreat. It must move out of the sanctuary into the living rooms of the lost. A dynamic personal evangelism program will put a church on the map of heaven and will make it come alive here on earth.

The evangelism program in the church itself includes (1) training people to evangelize and (2) actual evangelizing. The program must be first in the eyes and interest of the people of the congregation. The ideal church is one made up of members who are absolutely sold on the proposition that evangelism is the first business of the church, and who are eager to be actively and consistently involved in this business.

Evangelism not only wins the lost to Christ, but also wins the church to Christ. A church made up of large numbers of dedicated soul-winners will be spiritually alive, happy and growing. It will be a fellowship which is for its constituents a source of joy.

# WHAT EVANGELISM DOES FOR THE PEOPLE

First of all we observe the obvious — evangelism brings people to the Lord. Evangelism does much also for the evangelizers. There is no greater thrill on this earth than to be involved in bringing a soul to Christ. Traditionally (at least for the past several hundred years which cover the medieval and Protestant periods of history) the minister has in the main been the evangelistic task force of the church. The churches of the Restoration Movement, who sharply deny the validity of the clergy-laity dichotomy, have been slower than some of the conservative denominations to break with the unscriptural tradition of leaving the responsibility of evangelism up to the preachers.

Most any minister will testify that his greatest thrill in life is that of bringing a soul to Christ. Why should the ministry then be selfish with this thrill? Should not it be shared with all willing fellow-Christians? Once a Christian becomes addicted to the joy of soul-winning, he will never be the same again. He has found the way to real personal fulfillment and to Christian excellence through Christ and Christian service.

We have seen fairly new Christians grow in grace almost over-night because of their involvement in evangelism. We remember one man in Florida who won his own married daughter only one week after his baptism. He stated on the night of his conversion that this would be his first project.

In East Tennessee a young man who was experimenting heavily with drugs and sin in general accepted Christ when a team of callers encountered him on a Tuesday night. Five plastic bags of hardened model airplane glue were found in his room. Shortly after his baptism he came eagerly to volunteer as a trainee in evangelism. He went after many of his former associates. For several weeks thereafter he averaged bringing one soul a week to the Lord. He personally baptized several of them. He is now a dedicated ministerial student in a Bible college and is preaching at a mission church. The whole process from glue bags to preaching the Gospel involved less than a year and a half. What went on during that year or so? Two rounds of intensive work in evangelism - - four months as a trainee and four months as a trainer. In addition to these he involved himself almost daily in the wayside ministry, testifying wherever he went. Involvement in evangelism made the difference.

A definite goal in the evangelism training program is to turn out numbers of committed Christians who are continually and consistently evangelizing both in the announced calling program and in the wayside ministry. They tell the Good News on the job, in the car pool, in the neighborhood and wherever they go. When this happens we see the spirit of first century Christianity re-captured. God grant that it will happen everywhere in Christendom.

Often we have had our workers in evangelism call us or knock on our door late at night summoning us to the baptistry because they have prepared souls for "same hour of the night" obedience. Often the so-called "laymen" will do the baptizing themselves. In one case a young lady baptized another young lady. One elder said that at first it shocked him but then he asked himself, "Why not?" When the evangelizer who participates in the regular calling program also forms the habit of wayside witnessing, going every-where preaching the Word, he has indeed recaptured the spirit of the first century Christian.

Something wonderful happens to the church member who learns to be a soul winner. Every Christian owes it to himself to become involved in evangelism.

## REFLECTIONS

Jesus compared evangelism to sowing seeds (See Luke, Chapter Eight). It would be wonderful indeed to see all of our seeds of witnessing fall on fertile ground. Some, however, do fall by the wayside or on inferior soil. But even one soul, out of ten or one-hundred efforts, saved for eternity is worth it. Perhaps this parable could be used in answering excuses. Would not any prospect for salvation desire to be fertile ground?

Another consideration - - people often ask if we call by appointment. We seldom do. If a person has expressed a desire to be called upon, a phone appointment would be in order. Otherwise, the attempt to make appointments will more probably end in the frustration of the callers. The same people who would turn you down or put you off on the phone, may be won if encountered.

However, in calling without appointment, which we almost always do, the callers must be alert to the conditions of the moment in each home. If it is obviously a bad time to call, it is best to graciously retreat with the expression of a desire to return at a more suitable time. Witnessing under pressures, unless it is the pressure of the Holy Spirit, is usually a waste of time and may actually close the door to a future encounter. Always leave every home pleasantly and make every attempt to leave an open door.

Another volume could be written concerning particular situations encountered in witnessing. But the summary of such a subject matter can well be:

1. Always approach the call with much prayer.
2. Ask the Lord to lead with the presence of the Holy Spirit.
3. Use good common sense in every situation.
4. Stay with the subject of the Gospel outline, but be flexible.
5. Leave the final results to God and give Him the glory.

Wonderful things can happen in any church fellowship if the church leaders, and at least a fair percentage of the membership, will decide to go wholeheartedly into a church-wide personal evangelism program. If the Bible is true concerning a literal heaven and an eternal hell, and if the Gospel makes the difference, what more important emphasis may a church champion than that of evangelism?

Will you dare to break with the old Romanistic and Protestant traditions of institutional clergy-directed "churchanity"? Will you let God use your feet and your mouth to tell the Good News that Jesus saves?

*"For with the heart man believeth unto righteousness; and with the mouth confession is made unto salvation. For the scripture saith, Whosoever believeth on him shall not be ashamed. For there is no difference between the Jew and the Greek; for the same Lord over all is rich unto all that call upon him. For whosoever shall call upon the name of the Lord shall be saved. How then shall they call on him in whom they have not believed? and how shall they believe in him of whom they have not heard? and how shall they hear without a preacher? And how shall they preach, except they be sent? as it is written, How beautiful are the feet of them that preach the gospel of peace, and bring glad tidings of good things!"* (Romans 10:10-15).


How shall they believe unless they hear?
   God's great apostle said.
To lift the sinner from death's fear
   Christ Jesus came back from the dead.

Will you dare to believe this claim is true,
   Heaven's greatest story heard?
Will you dare obey His command to you,
   And proclaim His saving Word?

# INDEX

# What the Bible says they did to be saved.

Romans: 1:16—For I am not ashamed of the gospel of Christ: for it is the power of God unto salvation to every one that believeth; to the Jew first, and also to the Greek.

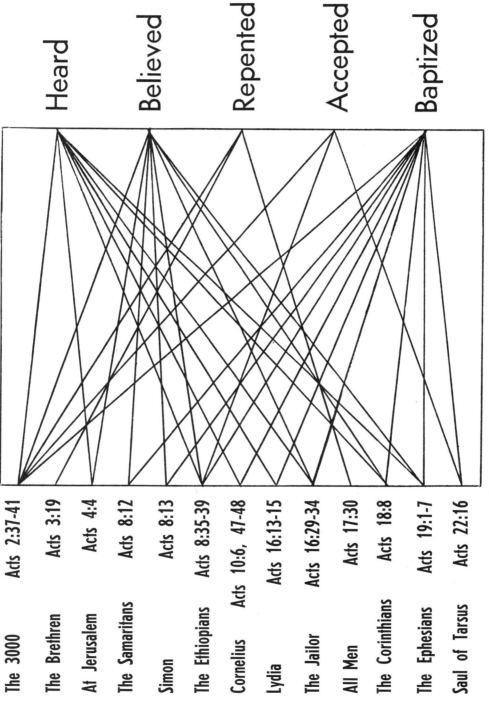

Heard

Believed

Repented

Accepted

Baptized

The 3000        Acts 2:37-41

The Brethren        Acts 3:19

At Jerusalem        Acts 4:4

The Samaritans        Acts 8:12

Simon        Acts 8:13

The Ethiopians        Acts 8:35-39

Cornelius        Acts 10:6, 47-48

Lydia        Acts 16:13-15

The Jailor        Acts 16:29-34

All Men        Acts 17:30

The Corinthians        Acts 18:8

The Ephesians        Acts 19:1-7

Saul of Tarsus        Acts 22:16

Were these people converted?
If so, what they had to do to be saved, you must do. God has but one plan of salvation, He is no "respecter of persons". What saved them, will save you.
Do you want to be saved and have the assurance that you are a child of God? Then do what the Bible tells you to do, and claim the promise.